# Praise for Awesome Blast

*Nili Salem's book is a shofar blast of spiritual enthusiasm.*

—**Rabbi David Wolpe**, Newsweek's Most Influential Rabbi in America, Rabbi Emeritus of Sinai Temple, Scholar at Harvard Divinity School, Author of Why Faith Matters

*Nili makes the Torah come alive in the most ecstatic ways. Energizing, visceral, and above all, life-giving.*

—**David Sacks**, Founder of Spiritual Tools for an Outrageous World, Former Writer for The Simpsons & Third Rock from the Sun

*Nili's voice is vibrant, soulful, and full of joy. With fearless spirit, she invites us into a journey of return that is alive, personal, and full of light.*

—**Rebbetzin Tanya HaLevi**, Director of Kol HaNearim

*Nili Salem is a master educator—always bringing an invigorating view to our everyday life. Her dedication to this book is sure to inspire with every page.*

—**Rabbi Chaim Levy**, Mashgiach, Eshel Sephardic Seminary; Founder, GoSephardic

*A wildly creative yet grounded way to approach the Jewish New Year—inspirational, real, accessible, and profound.*

—**Rabbi Avraham Arieh Trugman**, Director of Ohr Chadash, Author of 24 Books

*We are all in desperate need to receive a new breath of life. Through Nili's Torah on the Shofar, she allows us to do just that.*

—**Rav Shlomo Katz**, Musician and Rabbi, Kehilat Shirat David

*Happy is the nation that knows the shofar blast (Tehillim 89:16)—and happy is the person who learns from Nili Salem. Her joy and energy shine through every page.*

—**Esther Goldenberg**, Bestselling Author of The Desert Songs Trilogy

*Nili's Torah brings a deeper experience of Judaism than I ever imagined. Her teachings touch the soul in rare and powerful ways.*

—**Madison Margolin**, Author of Exile & Ecstasy, Co-Founder of DoubleBlind Magazine

*Nili Salem is the Jewish educator we've been waiting for—fiery, funny, deep, and unapologetically real. You'll laugh, cry, hear the shofar, and actually want to do Teshuva.*

—**Chaya Lester**, Psychotherapist, Educator & Author of Lit: Poems to Ignite Your Jewish Holidays

*As someone who lives and breathes the fusion of mysticism and music, Awesome Blast lit up my soul. A spiritual choose-your-own-adventure full of heart, humor, and holy fire.*

—**Erez Safar**, Author of the Light of the Infinite Series, DJ & Community Organizer

*Nili's passion for the Shofar is contagious. Each year, she helps me connect deeper to this mitzvah.*

—**Dave Mason**, Author of The Age of Prophecy Series

*A blast of brilliance—so far, this is shofar beyond the ordinary.*

—**Rabbi Harry Rosenberg**, Founder of Trippy.vc and iTribe

*Nili writes with her whole heart. She reframes the practice of Shofar with radiant clarity and fresh insight.*

—**Chen Malchut**, Dance-Movement Therapist, Teacher & International Consultant

# AWESOME BLAST

### 40 DAYS OF SHOFAR INTENTIONS, SOUL-HEALING & SPIRITUAL RETURN

A Choose Your Own Adventure Book:
to Blow Your Mind, Open Your Heart,
Invite you Believe in Yourself & the World Again,
and Help You Spiritually Prepare for the New Year

## NILI SALEM

Copyright © 2025 Nili Salem. All rights reserved.

No part of this publication may be reproduced, stored in a retrieval system, or transmitted in any form or by any means—electronic, mechanical, photocopy, recording, or otherwise—without prior written permission from the publisher, except in the case of brief quotations embodied in critical articles or reviews.

Published with love and strategy by Dr. Yael Maoz of Beverly House Press, who helps authors turn their message into a lasting legacy and a sustainable business.

Beverly House Press
304 E. Pine St. #1058
Lakeland, FL 33801
BeverlyHousePress.com

BEVERLY HOUSE

BeverlyHouse Press books are available at special discounts for bulk purchases in the United States by corporations, institutions, and other organizations. For more information, please contact markets@beverlyhousepress.com.

Cover, Internal Design, and Illustrations by the incredibly talented, humble and holy **David Hillel**. Find out more about David's work at reshimu.com.

Edited by the epic and wise **Elijah Goldenberg**.

Cover photograph by **Ronen Jembe**
On Lara Weinberg's Soulfull Tours

ISBN: 978-1-957466-19-4

## To the Barak Raviv Foundation

From the moment Barak walked into my classroom in Gondar, Ethiopia, I was blessed with an angel. Whether it was making Jewish star necklaces for the Lost Tribes, building orphanages in West Africa, sending me on *shlichut* to Papua, gifting me studio time to produce "*The Song of Shabbas*," or standing strong in support of Israel during times of war—you have been a source of life, faith, and possibility.

You have enabled me, and so many others, not just to survive, but to dream, to build, and to thrive.
You are the most magical of co-creators, and for twenty years now, your support has been woven through my life's greatest achievements. I owe so much of who I have become to your faith in me and your generosity.

My mother was one of your biggest admirers—and that says everything, because she saw straight into people's souls.

May God bless you, your beautiful Indre, and your precious daughters with the sweetest blessings of this life.
May you continue to be pillars of joy, kindness, strength, and light in the community and in the world.

Blessing you with health, wealth, honor, *nachas*, bliss, love, laughter, and infinite abundance.

Thank you—with all my heart.

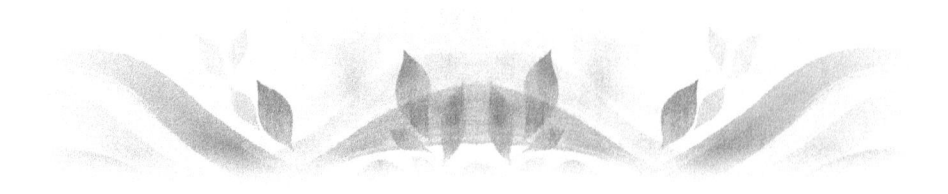

### In memory of Noach ben Avraham z'l

For the sweetest, highest, symphony-filled soul ascension of **Noach ben Avraham**, z'l.
A most precious man, husband, and father—whose physical form now rests just feet away from where my mother's physical form rests. Surely no coincidence... treasures buried side by side to illuminate the Heavens for their families, and for the world.

And to his anonymous wife, **Dvora bat Yosefa v'Yehudah**—an angel in human form—the most generous, the sweetest, the most kind. With a light so luminous it fills a room, and with a humility so deep it takes up no space at all.

You have truly been an angel and a mama-figure to me. Just writing these words brings tears to my eyes.
You are an unexpected, precious gift in my life, and I am so grateful for your love and support.

May you be blessed with the sweetest, richest life, *ad meah v'esrim* (until 120 years), filled with health, joy, and light.
May we dance again with our loved ones at the time of *techiyat hameitim* (the revival of the dead)—may it be soon—and may we all dance together to the Temple, in health, joy, and wholeness.

Thank you—with all my heart.

## Harvey & Jackie Barnett Family

of Highland Park, Illinois

Yasher Koach to Nili Salem for all her wonderful work, energy, and ruach on behalf of Klal Yisrael.

---

Harvey and Jackie have been my parents' dearest friends for over 50 years—true mensches of the highest kind. They have stood by our family through thick and thin, embodying loyalty, wisdom, and love. True role models in every sense.

They have raised the most beautiful family, and have given so much—quietly, generously—to countless souls around them. They are upstanding, moral, honest, clever, funny, and simply luminous human beings.

Just knowing that my father has a best friend like Harvey is one of the greatest gifts a daughter could ask for. Truly. Baruch Hashem.

I am deeply, endlessly grateful—not only for the way you have stood by him, but also for the unwavering support you have shown me and my endless projects over the years.

May your family be blessed beyond measure.
May your Torah learning be blessed and ever-deepened,
And may everything you touch be blessed with goodness and joy, *ad meah v'esrim* (until 120 years and beyond).

Thank you for being you.
Thank you for being there for us.

## To the Anonymous Family in Los Angeles

There are tzaddikim, and then there are tzaddikim.

This young, humble family lives so purely aligned with their values—with kindness, generosity, humility, and the Torah itself—that it is truly awe-inspiring.

You are role models, friends, supporters, and community builders… and beyond all that, you are simply really cool.

You know who you are.

Thank you for all the support, encouragement, and light you have offered me through the years.

I am deeply, endlessly grateful for your existence.

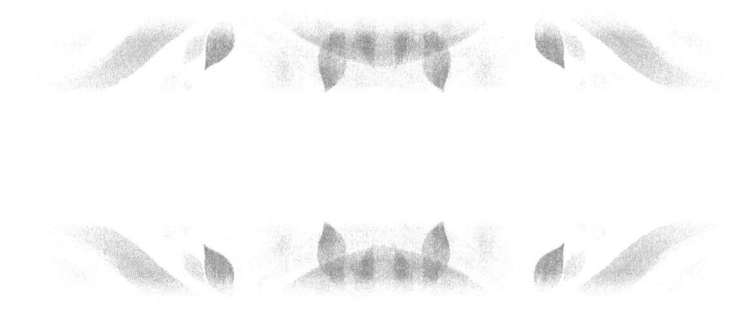

## Thank you to Chana and Dave Mason, and Madison Margolin

Local book wizards and true mensches,
who so generously gave me their time, guidance, and invaluable advice as I set out to write my first book.

A priceless gift from accomplished authors.

Thank you, truly—and may all of your work be blessed infinite-fold and beyond.

# The Juicy Contents

In Thanks to the One ........................................................ 1

CHOOSE YOUR OWN ADVENTURE!
Aka How to Navigate this Book.......................................... 4

The Main Point of the Book and of your Life
(and of Our Entire Role here on Earth) ................................ 7

The Subway Story ........................................................ 20

## The Month of Elul

The Energies of the Month of Elul ....................................... 25

| Av 30 | | The Power of Renewal ................................. 30 |
| | | The Very First Shofar ................................... 33 |
| Elul 1 | | The Intimate Bond, The French Kiss, & the Magen David.................................... 37 |
| Elul 2 | | Mindfulness & A Spiritual Accounting of the Soul ................................... 39 |

○ ○ ○

Now is the time to begin *Nili's Famous Fun Practical Guide to Doing Basic Tshuva!* on PAGE 182

○ ○ ○

| | | | |
|---|---|---|---|
| Elul 3 | \| | Manifestation, the Messiah & Limiting Beliefs . | 42 |
| Elul 4 | \| | Sound Healing & Frequencies | 45 |
| Elul 5 | \| | Listening & Intuition: The Keys to Personal Peace, Peace in the Home, and Peace in the World | 50 |
| Elul 6 | \| | Self Improvement, Self-Respect, the Patriarchs & a Mind-blowing Definition of Tshuva | 58 |
| Elul 7 | \| | Breath Work & Spiritual Rapé: | 62 |
| Elul 8 | \| | Birth & Surrender | 64 |
| Elul 9 | \| | The Portal of Female Anatomy | 67 |
| Elul 10 | \| | Splitting of the Sea & the Shofar | 70 |
| Elul 11 | \| | Amniotic Fluid, the Womb, & God in Liturgy | 72 |
| Elul 12 | \| | Synesthesia & Tripping Out | 75 |
| Elul 13 | \| | Love & Ultimate Unity | 79 |
| Elul 14 | \| | Jericho—Letting Down Your Walls | 81 |
| Elul 15 | \| | The Greatest Ego Death | 85 |
| Elul 16 | \| | Snakes, Ayahuasca, & Kundalini Rising!?! | 89 |
| Elul 17 | \| | The Shofar and the Baal Shem Tov | 97 |
| Elul 18 | \| | The Primordial Scream | 114 |
| Elul 19 | \| | The Silent Scream | 106 |
| Elul 20 | \| | The Primal Scream—I Dare You! | 108 |
| Elul 21 | \| | When Words Don't Do It | 110 |
| Elul 22 | \| | Wait, We Talk About the Shofar Three Times a Day? | 112 |

| Elul 23 | How is a Shofar Made & What We Can Learn from the Process?........................................114 |
| Elul 24 | Shofar Fun Facts ............................................116 |
| Elul 25 | Creation, Co-Creation & The 'Law of Attraction' ..120 |
| Elul 26 | A Hammer for My Hardened Heart aka Holy Soul Surgery................................ 123 |
| Elul 27 | Heartstrings ............................................. 126 |
| Elul 28 | Why the Shofar is also the first and also the 'Last' ....................................... 128 |
| Elul 29 | Crowning the King & Circle Consciousness ..... 131 |

## The Month of Tishrei

*It's the final countdown...
dahtah dah-tah, dah duh
dah dah tah tah*

Prologue to Rosh Hashanah,
the 10 Days of Tshuva, & Yom Kippur Teachings ...................135

The Days of Wet Cement ................................................ 136

The Skyscraper Metaphor................................................ 138

The Energies of the Month of Tishrei ............................... 140

| Tishrei 1 | Can I Bedazzle My Shofar?.......................... 146 |
| Tishrei 2 | What if There is a Crack in My Shofar?.......... 148 |
| Tishrei 3 | Turn It Upwards ....................................... 152 |
| Tishrei 4 | Maybe We Don't Have to Try So Hard? ............155 |
| Tishrei 5 | It Doesn't Have to Be Perfect, Just Don't Give Up .......................................157 |
| Tishrei 6 | The Shofar Represents Strength ................... 159 |

| Tishrei 7 | Wait, We Do Our Holiest Work Through the Physical? ................................................. 161 |
| Tishrei 8 | Kabbalistic Intentions on Balance, Healing, and Unification: An Advanced Teaching ......... 163 |
| Tishrei 9 | Preparing for Kol Nidre: a Battle Call on the Inner Critic .................... 166 |
| Tishrei 10 | You're Already Forgiven ............................. 171 |

Conclusion and Preparation for Sukkot ........................... 174

Sukkot—Last Teaching and All You Need to Know ............... 180

Nili's Famous Practical Guide to Doing Basic Tshuva! ......... 182

Further Resources .................................................... 211

Dictionary of Hebrew Words ....................................... 212

More Shofar Videos ............... 220

About the Author ................. 223

*Most Hebrew words in the text are in italics so you know you can refer to the dictionary in the back.*

# In Thanks to the One

Hi Hashem.

Thank You Hashem.

What a bizarre and fun blessing to be obsessed with the Shofar. Thank You!

What a wonderful blessing to think about Mashiach so very often, and to get to share that with the readers, my sweet brothas and sistas of humanity. Thank You!

Thank You for my life. Thank You for the challenges. Thank You for the joy, the glee, the creativity, the courage, and the dedication to sit and write and make this happen.

Thank You for my computer, my fingers, my brain, my eyes, the time, the resources, the education, and teachers. Thank You for bringing me to *Morah* Leah Golomb, whose passion, faith, coolness and realness inspired a huge part of my Torah journey.

Thank You for my parents who dedicated so much of their lives to provide me with a Jewish education and a meaningful upbringing. *L'chaim* to my mama Roen *z'l*, may her memory be a blessing, who is probably doing super-funky art projects and having a beer with God.

Shofar at the Magbit Gala, Beverly Hills

### Awesome Blast

To my dad, Dr. Don, aka the GOAT (greatest of all time), for supporting me in the first few years of this book's inception and for always giving me the Priestly Blessing!

Thank You for my ancestors who paved the way.

Thank You for my family and my close friends who held and hold me, make me laugh, and deal with their own embarrassment when I show up to random places with the Shofar or ask them to film. Rhiana, Dan, Jo, Steph, Shaindel, Chen, Lany, Shari, Tzofia, Mishpachat Balter, and others, they know who they are.

And thank You Hashem for creating Jenna Chana-Netina Zadaka and having her tell me that I need to write this book. It was her encouragement that kicked off this whole writing initiative.

Thank You for my social-media friends whose feedback has given me so much encouragement and many of whom contributed financially to support the original Elul Shofar video series.

Thank you for Esther Goldenberg, my human angel, for connecting me to my creative, brilliant, and chill editor Elijah Goldenberg. I could not have put this book out without them.

Thank You Hashem for bringing the Great Day for us all, *I am SO excited to party in peace and joy in Yerushalayim all together!* WOW! Yayyyy! Thank You!

Hashem, may this book please be a blessing to all those that dabble or dive into it. May something in it be the thing that someone needed to hear. May its study bring friends, couples, families and communities closer. May it be the reason people share meaningful conversation over weekday and Shabbat meals. May it help people prepare for the High Holidays. And ultimately may it help everyone find even greater belief in themselves so we have an epic world of people that know their own precious shining power, so we can unite and shine it all over the whole darn Universe, asap! *AMEN!*

And... can You please sound the Great Shofar NOW?! Thank You Hashem.

# CHOOSE YOUR OWN ADVENTURE!
## Aka How to Navigate this Book

**1. THE THOROUGH READER:** You'll probably read it cover to cover—If you are anything like me and love being thorough, you'll want to start at the beginning and read through to the last page. Be warned, you might just catch the Shofar bug & obsession with Mashiach too.

**2. PREPARE ME MENTALLY FOR THE HOLIDAYS READER:** This is for the reader that wants an essay-a-day or devotional to get them focused for holidays, but isn't in the mood to get out the pen and paper. Essays start on page 25, read an essay a day all the way through til Yom Kippur. Good job, I like your focus.

**3. I WANT TO USE THE BOOK TO GO DEEPER WITH MY PARTNER, STUDENTS, OR WITH MY FAMILY AT MY DINNERTABLE:** Perfect. You can read an essay-a-day together and then turn to the Reflection Questions Companion Guide available at awesomeblastbook.com/guide.

*Wow! It's an entire educational resource companion guide to go along with this book?! For adults and kids?! Praise the Lawd this really is an Awesome Blast! ;)*

CHOOSE YOUR OWN ADVENTURE! Aka How to Navigate this Book

Turn to the further resources section on page 211 for the Link Tree QR code. The questions can be used as food for thought, discussion starters, or as journal prompts.

**4.** I WANT TO DO NILI'S FAMOUS TSHUVA PROCESS! Wonderful. I'll be doing it alongside of you. Doing this process truly helps me feel that I have done some honest reflection, and allows me to show up in *shul* feeling prepared to bring in a new year! Check out the *Tshuva* Guide on page 182 and get your calendars out so you can schedule the process in!

Shofar on a Plane, Raw & Unedited

## Disclaimer about my choice of referring to God as "He"

Why did I make that choice for the book? Simplicity. And also, not to freak out our more traditional readers. Creating change takes time and patience, and hey, they already picked up a book with a chick blowing a Shofar on it's cover so that is a good start, lol.

By the way, I called a Chareidi Posek to check if there would be a problem with calling God a She, and his answer was, 'only if they have a problem with how the Kabbalah and the Zohar view things!'

Does it represent a personal view that God should be seen as a fundamentally masculine force? Nope.

Do I long for, and wish to contribute to a world in which both the human and Divine Feminine/Masculine are acknowledged, respected, and appreciated? Yup.

Is that why I wrote this disclaimer? Yup.
Thanks for understanding.

Big love to the stunning sistas bravely startin' to shine, to the Feminine Rising, and to Circle Consciousness.

With mad respect to the brothas doin' their work too. Thanks for holding us. We mamash need you. Shine on warriors.

Jah bless. Jewstafari, One love, sista' Nee

# The Main Point of the Book and of your Life
## (and of Our Entire Role here on Earth)

"Can you explain why you have a Shofar?," a woman politely asked yesterday while I waited for the train in Tel Aviv. I carry a Shofar because practically speaking, who knows, maybe it will be needed right now to call out the Great Day![1]

And I carry a Shofar so people will continue to ask why I am carrying a Shofar.

I come prepared with the Shofar spiritually speaking because it is a deep reminder of the goal of world-peace.

This goal isn't an airy-fairy hope of the trippy-hippie-vegetarian-peace-and-love Jews like myself who love campfires, crystals and incense. It is so much deeper than that. It is a visual reminder of the meaning and purpose of our lives. I will explain...

Shofar at the Donut Shop in Vegas

By this point I am notorious in the community for bringing my huge Shofar with me wherever I go. And if I may add, I am pretty good at getting quite the powerful sound out of it!

## Awesome Blast

*OK, let's admit it, it's only three sounds, but I am REALLLLY good at those three sounds! God blessed me with some serious lungs!*

So it is common that when people see me carrying this three-foot twister, that they ask me to blow the shofar for them. I made a deal with God that whenever someone asks me that I say yes.

And believe me, saying yes isn't always easy on my ego. Sometimes it means I will be calling a lot of attention to myself in situations in which I am just not in the mood for it. Sometimes it is actually quite embarrassing.

*Not only is it super loud and a show-stopper, but my cheeks blow up and my face turns purple in the process!* Sometimes it means I will end up awkwardly blowing the Shofar on Beverly Boulevard in Beverly Hills outside of fancy cafes. But… that is my deal with God. If they ask, I do it. It feels like my special personal *avoda*, my service of God.

And I don't *just* have a deal with God, I also make a deal with those that request to hear it: 'I play and you pray'. As long as they hear the sound of the Shofar they should pray for *Geulah Shlema B'Rachamim,*[2] for the Messianic era to come, now, in full glory, and that it should unfold with Divine Compassion.

*Can you imagine the reactions I get when I make that prayer request as if it's the most normal and obvious thing in the world?*

Anyhow, now that you know the background of what it's like to carry around a huge Shofar, I want to share a story… I recently showed up to a big community Chanukah party in Los Angeles with my Shofar. So there I am; decked out in

## The Main Point of the Book and of your Life

a glittery dress, a sparkling headband, shimmering jewelry, and shiny eye-shadow, and carrying my Shofar over my shoulder. *One of my greatest joys is creatively making our precious tradition come sparkling back to life, so I regularly try to dress according to the holiday or the weekly Torah portion... so for me Chanukah time means I get to wear as many shiny things as possible!*

This particular Chanukah party was actually an amazing event that my sister Danielle put on called "Dreidelmania," which was her brainchild and attempt to gather the community and see if they can break the Guiness Book of World Records' record for number of *dreidels* spinning at one time. Hundreds and hundreds of people gathered in a fancy hall under massive chandeliers for the main event.

There was a big count-down until record-breaking-dreidel-spin, famous musicians gave presentations, and even an all-star NBA player came to hype up the scene! I was there to support my sister, so I walked up to her colleague-Rabbi and I said, by the way, if you want me to blow the Shofar I would be happy to! I thought it would be a great way to add grandeur to the ceremony, or even just to call the attention to the masses if the organizers needed, as there were so many children running around and so much general noise with all of the people present.

But the Rabbi, *who, by the way I totally love and is my buddy,* looked at me like I was TOTALLY nuts. His neck jolted back, his face turned red and his eyebrows furrowed down with the most confused expression on his face. I inferred from his reaction that his response meant 'no thank you,' and I

## Awesome Blast

didn't even wait for the response before I politely curtsied and walked away, lol.

I could read in his eyes what he may have said if any words managed to leave his mouth... 'Why on planet Earth would we want you to play the Shofar at a Chanukah event Nili??? It is not Rosh Hashanah![3] Are you confused? Why would you ask me that?... wrong holiday sister."

But in my humble opinion, it was not the wrong holiday for the Shofar. In fact, it is never the wrong holiday for the Shofar. And the truth is, there is never even a wrong day or moment for the Shofar. (Of course except for on Shabbat when the Shofar is considered off-limits because it is not appropriate to carry or blow a Shofar on Shabbat according to Jewish law.)[4]

Anyhow, the Rabbi's reaction was actually so normal, and that is part of the reason why I decided to write this book. His was only one of many such reactions. I often hear the sounds of whispers behind me as I walk by, at first exclaiming, 'look it's a Shofar!,' and then 'wait, but it is not Rosh Hashanah.'

We have been waiting for 5786 years for the Great Day. Not just waiting, but working, with every day of our lives, with every *mitzvah*, with every act of loving-kindness, every coin placed in a charity box, with every page of Torah wisdom turned, with every restrained word of gossip, with every character trait improved, every addiction curbed, every diaper changed with love, and every social media post that unites towards a goal of peace for the whole world.[5]

Bringing the Great Day for the whole world is the Jewish mission and purpose in life. To bring about a time in which we all acknowledge that we are One. One family

## The Main Point of the Book and of your Life

of humanity. Brothas and sistas meant to relate to each other in righteousness, with care for each others' mental, spiritual, emotional, and physical well being. The vision is all of us gathering together at the Third Temple, or House of Love and Prayer for All Nations,[6] in Jerusalem, to celebrate peace, love, and the Master of the Universe—Who was busy loving us the whole time. Hopefully by the time you read this, House of Love and Prayer for All Nations will already be standing here real and shining!

We know from the book of Yeshayahu 27:13 that " it shall be on that day that a great Shofar shall be sounded, and those who were lost in the land of Ashur and those who were banished in the land of Mitzrayim shall come and bow down to the Lord on the holy mountain in Yerushalayim." In other words, we know that one day we will see this Great Day, and this Great Day is announced by a Shofar.

The question is, *do YOU believe it?*

Do you believe that the time will come?

Do you believe that the time can come in your lifetime?

How about today?

Well, I believe it to the core of my bones and in every cell and fiber of my being. And I believe that if it *is* coming, that it might well just come RIGHT NOW!, or today, or at any given wedding or holiday party that I might be attending with my Shofar in tow. There is no wrong time for the end of all human suffering,[7] for world peace,[8] and therefore there is no wrong time to call out on the Shofar in hopes that maybe, just maybe, *that* will be the call that is heard that announces the Great Day.

## Awesome Blast

Now just to make it clear, I have no delusions that I am some version of Elijah the Prophet.[9] I *do* have dreams that someday I will get to play the Shofar at the Third Temple[10] in Jerusalem, because why not?!

And although I completely understand the simple confusion of that sweet Rabbi who looked at me probably thinking, 'gosh I thought you knew about Judaism and that is just the WRONG holiday,' I await the day where every Rabbi and every Jew and every human understands why I would offer the call of the Shofar in any given significant moment.

Now, let's get to the more important question. Not why *I* believe in the real coming of a Great Day/Era that we can hasten and manifest even through our belief, but whether or not *you* believe it, and why you may or may not want to.

One reason… What is your other option?

Not to believe it?

Okay… how is that working for you?

What beliefs does that lead you to?

That there is no hope for humanity, that the world, the globe, and everything is going to s-h-i…?

That we have been left alone by a God who made the world and then left it to creatures who might just destroy it because He thought it was clever to give us free will and we chose selfishness?

That there may be a God but He[11] doesn't care about us, how things turn out, nor our efforts?

That there might be a God but He is not a Good God?

The truth is, I don't have proof for you.

## The Main Point of the Book and of your Life

I am just blessed that I have always believed in God and that God is GOOD.[12]

But I continue to choose to believe it, and remind myself of it on the regular, especially when I am in struggle.

You know why?

Because I think deep inside, each one of us *knows* that we are good, or else we wouldn't get so upset when people think poorly of us or our intentions. And we are made in the image of God. So... if we are inherently, deeply, profoundly good... well... then...

And if God is GOOD, then I don't think He played some big cruel joke on us called: 'watch what a beautiful world I can create and you can F up...'

or

'enjoy the demise, suckers'

or

'try as you may there is no hope, you'll never be good enough nor get it right'

or

'all the effort and prayer is for nothing, but that was funny to watch.'

Nope.

Now, I get it. The average intellectual has reason to suspect that things aren't looking so good. Wars galore, environmental disasters left and right, political corruption, cultural values looking more and more like those of Sodom and Gemorah, open antisemitism, the cost of living going up, the *Shidduch* crisis… and the list goes on…

While this life can be a tragic, tumultuous and painful ride, it is also wonderful, glorious, gorgeous, and most importantly, all of our efforts are in fact building towards something incredible.

As Reb David Sacks, spiritual leader of the Happy Minyan in Los Angeles, says: if it doesn't look good, the story isn't over.

He likes to shout it, and so do I.

## THE STORY ISN'T OVER! THE STORY ISN'T OVER! DON'T GIVE UP! THE STORY ISN'T OVER!

Have many people come and gone and not seen a Great Day? Yes. Might we also? Yes.

I'll reiterate, I do believe it could come as soon as *this very moment*, and most of the great Chassidic masters of our time do as well. But at some point, us, or our children, or our children's children *will* see it come to fruition. The truth is we have already witnessed many of the Biblical prophecies unfold before our very eyes….[13] but we can save that for another book. Basically, the stats are looking good for God and His prophets' words coming true!

And if I die, and I was wrong, this book was a farce and I just fall apart into the worms and dust of the earth with no ongoing soul-experience, I will never have known the difference. I may have missed some afternoons of Sunday football, some drinks at the bar, and I could have had my dignity those times where schlepping and blowing a Shofar was super embarrassing…. But I certainly won't regret having lived a life with my eyes-on-the-prize of the most

## The Main Point of the Book and of your Life

meaningful, beautiful, loving, and hopeful goal of all time... doing our individual parts in bringing the Great Day.

I sure don't regret keeping my eyes on the prize now. And, for the skeptics, if I do die and disintegrate into nothing forever, I won't have consciousness and therefore I wouldn't be able to have an experience of regret anyhow!

OK so let's review...

We know intuitively that we are good.

Therefore we can deduce that God is Good.

And also, the euphoria of love, the awe from nature, the experience of music, the bliss of babies, the luxurious taste of food, and the miracles of the body are just too incredible and too stunning not to have come from an extraordinarily Good Creator. But hey, if you don't feel it... *'you do you boo.'*

BUT! If God *is* GOOD and this *isn't* some cruel cosmic joke, it is surely likely that a Great Day is coming.

Therefore, we call out with the Shofar to remind us of this upcoming era, of the hope that is ours to hold, and of our role in dedicating our lives to that goal.

I carry a Shofar because you never know when that moment will be. I carry a Shofar because it helps remind me and others of this collective goal that in turn gives essential meaning and profound purpose to our lives.

Great!

We're on track.

*So why spend all of the month of Elul learning about the Shofar?*

## Awesome Blast

*Why read this book in general?*

Well for starters, the teachings are freaking fascinating and it is mind-blowing to notice how much a part of our tradition the Shofar is and has been, especially when most of us thought it is only a Rosh Hashanah custom. Additionally, all this Shofar and 'Great Day' talk might be somewhat new to you. Or even if you have heard about the Shofar and Mashiach your whole life, the concept could still just be dead or boring to you.

But considering you are reading this, you are probably ready to open your heart to new Shofar wisdom, and any new wisdom that one wishes to truly possess must not only be understood, but integrated.

Integration requires consciousness,[14] or simply put, paying attention to it. By keeping the spiritual ideas about the Shofar close to our hearts for a month, surely some of the teachings will drop in and affect our consciousness.

My teacher Morah Leah Golomb often shares the following teaching from the Kotzker Rebbe that begins with a question. Why is it that in the paragraphs of the daily *Shema* prayer, the words are, "you shall place these words upon your heart?"[15] Why "upon"? Don't we want words of faith to go *into* our hearts? So she answers, yes, we do want the words to go into our hearts.... but! But we are human... and we cannot expect from ourselves the highest levels of intention, focus and spiritual success every day. So what do we do instead? Everyday when we recite the words from the prayer book, we put the words of the *Shema* UPON our hearts with just a reasonably drab and *neeeeed-another-coffee amount of daily kavanah*, or spiritual-intention. And then, one fine day,

## The Main Point of the Book and of your Life

when our prayers are strong, *(or we are having PMS, lol, you feel me sisters)* and our emotions are high, we pray and our heart breaks open. And then allllll of the prayers that have been stacked UPON our hearts fall IN and find their place deep inside our hearts and our beings.

So here we have it.

40 Shofar essays for the 40 days between Elul and Yom Kippur to wake us up to the New Year.

Or perhaps that was too simple.

What I really, actually mean is as follows. I don't just want people to have another 'New Year, New You' tool or moment of inspiration to make their coming year the best possible year. Or also, maybe you are picking this book up in the middle of the year.

So what is my real passion connected to this topic?

Dr. Viktor Frankl said it best—meaning is the most important thing in our lives.

The consciousness of the Shofar and its call to the "Great Day" is a consciousness of meaning and purpose. The blessing of living my life deeply believing that Mashiach could come any moment is that gift of purpose.[16] Every day I wake up knowing I am here for a reason and it leads me to deeply wanting to infuse my life's actions with that meaning. There is no greater blessing I could ask for. This consciousness fills me with an unbreakable hope in God, for the world and for myself, it reinforces my faith, and empowers me to believe in my own importance. That is huge.

So heck yeah I am gonna rock my huge Shofar. Even at Chanukah parties!

## Awesome Blast

I am so honored that you chose to dive into these meaningful topics with me.

Thank you for going on this Shofar journey with me. May it be a blessing of awakened consciousness in you, and may that consciousness infuse your inner power and passion to shine your truest light and gifts into the world.

Ok, let's dive into some super seriously yummy torahs...

## Notes

1. The Amidah Prayer: Blessing of Ingathering of Exiles. The tenth blessing reads: "Sound the great Shofar for our freedom, raise the banner to gather our exiles and gather us together from the four corners of the earth. Blessed are You, Hashem, Who gathers in the dispersed of His people, Israel."
2. The Talmud extensively discusses the coming of the Messiah (Sanhedrin 98a—99a) and describes a period of freedom and peace, which will be the time of ultimate goodness for the Jews. Tractate Sanhedrin contains a long discussion of the events leading to the coming of the Messiah.
3. Numbers 29:1—The Torah refers to Rosh Hashanah as the "day of the (*Shofar*) blast."
4. Alter Rebbe's Shulchan Aruch, Orach Chaim 588:4.
5. Habakuk 2:3, Zephaniah 3:8, Jeremiah 31:16, Isaiah 30:18, Isaiah 56:1, *Targum Yehonathan*, and *Bereishit Rabba* 98:14, *Midrash Tehilim* 40:114, *Pesikta Rabaty* 35:2 (ed. Friedmann, ch. 34), Rambam's 13 Principles of Faith, Malachi 3:1, and see article on Chabad.org entitled "Awaiting Mashiach" for a full explanation of the Jewish idea of waiting for and anticipating Mashiach every day.
6. Isaiah 56:7—"Even them I will bring to My holy mountain, and make them joyful in My house of prayer. Their burnt offerings and their sacrifices will be accepted on My altar; for My house shall be called a house of prayer for all nations."
7. Ezekiel 38:16.

# The Main Point of the Book and of your Life

8. Isaiah 11:11-12; Jeremiah 23:8; 30:3; Hosea 3:4-5.

9. Malachi 3:4—24.

10. Maimonides, Mishneh Torah (Laws of Kings 11:1).

11. God does not 'have a gender,' and the Divine Masculine and Divine Feminine are in partnership, but I will be referring to God as a He simply for ease and language limitations.

12. Exodus 32:10, Psalms 34, 100, & 159.

13. The Rebirth of Israel as a Nation (Isaiah 66:8).

    The Ingathering of the Jewish People (Ezekiel 36:24), Zechariya 13,8, Talmud (Megilla 17a), Midrash Tanchuma P. Shoftim 9.

    The Revival of the Hebrew Language (Zephaniah 3:9).

    The Land Becoming Fertile Again (Isaiah 27:6).

    Jerusalem Under Jewish Control (Zechariah 8:7-8), Maimonides, Teshuva 8, 7; 9, 2, based upon Brachot 34b.

    Jerusalem as a Burdensome Stone (Zechariah 12:3).

    The Rebuilding of Cities and Villages (Ezekiel 36:10-11).

    The Desert Blooming (Isaiah 35:1).

    The Worldwide Impact of Israel (Isaiah 42:6).

    The Survival of Israel Against All Odds (Amos 9:15).

    "There is no more 'revealed/clear sign/time' than that which is written (Yechezkel 36, 8), 'And you, mountains of Israel, give forth your branches, and carry forth your fruit, for My Nation of Israel is coming/returning soon'. Rashi explains that when the Land of Israel (barren for so long) will return to produce fruit abundantly, that is the clearest sign that the return of the Jewish Nation is near. The flourishing modern Land of Israel, barren just 100 years ago, speaks for itself. According to the OEC, The Observatory of Economic Complexity, an online data visualization and distribution platform for international trade data, in 2023, Israel exported $258M in Citrus, making it the 16th largest exporter of Citrus in the world.

14. Tononi, G. An information integration theory of consciousness. *BMC Neurosci* 5, 42 (2004).

15. Deuteronomy 11:18-23.

16. "Yeshuat Hashem k'heref ayin—the salvation and deliverance from evil occasioned by God's will is but an eye blink away from us." Brachos 2b, Shabbos 34b, Yerushalmi Brachot 3a, Midrash Lekach Tov on Esther 4:17.

# The Subway Story

Reb Shlomo Carlebach shared this sweetest story. I have heard many variations of it, so this is a composite of the versions I have heard.

One day there was a young man on the Subway in New York. It was a regular day and he was on his way to work. But something happened, his eyes caught the gaze of a young woman on the other side of the subway car, and without question he knew that this was his soulmate. Their eyes locked, they had tunnel vision, and all of the other passengers that were packed in around them seemed to fade away.

It was love at first sight. His whole body felt weak. But he didn't know what to do with himself, he was shy, and afraid to approach a total stranger. What was he supposed to do? He lowered his eyes and blushed and tried to muster the courage to go over to her but he was totally overwhelmed.

A couple minutes went by and he knew he couldn't pass us this opportunity, so he got up and began to make his way through the crowd. Just as he made it to her, he realized that this was her stop, and she was about to exit the car! Hi... I... umm... can I please have your number? I just need to see you again... she

Shofar at the Peterson Car Museum

# The Subway Story

was in agreement but shouted her number as the crowds of people pushing past whisked her off the car.... And much to his dismay, he only caught the area code 917...

He pushed to try to get off as well but didn't succeed... he got off at the next stop and tried to get back on a train in the other direction but she was nowhere to be found. He was devastated!

But he couldn't let her go. So every day he went back to that stop around the same time and waited for her. When that didn't work he began to drive around the entire 917 area code looking for her on the streets. Weeks went by and he searched for her, weeks turned into months and months turned into years. *And Reb Shlomo would add that he searched for 2,000 years...* But he never forgot her. One day on his drive to search for her he was so caught up in daydreaming he ran a few red lights and it wasn't long before the cops pulled him over. He had run so many lights this was immediately assigned as a court case. He was so bummed.

When the date finally came for his court case, he entered the room with his head hung, but as he approached the podium, he raised his eyes... and in total disbelief and shock, he came to realize who the judge was... no other than the woman from the subway car!!!! He was filled with emotion... fear, joy, tears.. And she.... She too was overwhelmed, recalling exactly who he was, and having experienced the same longing over the years. First he began to beg and plead his case... your Honor, I am so sorry, please let me explain...

But she quickly hushed him, knocked down the gavel and announced that court would go to recess. Everyone left the room except for him. He ran up to her, she hurried down off the podium, and they fell into embrace. She said...there is time for judgment... but first... first I am just so overwhelmingly glad to see you! Not a day has gone by since I haven't thought about you... I have been waiting and waiting... What took you so long???

As you may have inferred, the woman in the story, the judge, is meant to represent God, and the man in the story, the Jewish people. The Jewish people were exiled from our Land 2,000 years ago and have never stopped thinking about God. We search for God high and low, everywhere we go. And yes, while God is the Judge that we face on Rosh Hashanah,[1] God isn't just a judge. God is the One who loves us the most...[2] Who is with us constantly, madly in love, and overwhelmingly joyful when we return.

*Can you imagine if you met God right now and He looked at you like He with tears in His 'eyes,' overjoyed to see you, and the first question He lovingly asked you was, 'what took you so long?' Ohhh sweet vulnerable longing! YUM.*

The "Subway Story" goes beautifully with the concept that there is a process to the *chaggim*:

The process is that Elul, the month in which God is said to be so close,[3] is like the time period of romantic partners wooing each other.

Rosh Hashanah, the day on which we choose God,[4] is likened to an engagement.

Yom Kippur is likened to the wedding day. Just as in the process on a Jewish wedding day we dress in white, we are cleansed of all sin, we fast and then feast, and enter into the *Yichud* room with our partner to solidify the marriage, just as we do in the final prayer service of Yom Kippur, *Neilah*.[5] When describing the process to my students I always pause the class and invite them to watch loving blubbering groom videos on YouTube, in order to help my students really tune in to what God must 'feel' like as He watches his bride, Am Yisrael, come up the aisle, aka show up for Yom Kippur. *If you really want to rewire any religious trauma of the punishing God who damns people to hell, I highly recommend that you also pause here and watching a few emotional grooms see their brides walk up the aisle... get a taste of what God might actually feel like when He sees YOU show up for the holidays... it might create some awesome new neural pathways, fo' sho!*

And finally, Sukkot, and its seven days of celebration mimics the *sheva brachot*, or the seven days of celebration that Jewish couples participate in after their wedding. A time of great joy and rejoicing in the sacred union that was just formed!

So yes, there is time for judgment, for the hard conversations between couples. It is a must for reconnection and growth. But first, when we approach the High Holidays we must know what a beautiful, loving, romantic, caring re/union it truly is. Now with *that* context we have set the stage. God is not some harsh judge[6] in the sky and we are not some low-lives who need to come groveling. We are soulmates,[7] falling in love anew and/or trying to repair any hurt and distance so that we can come even closer than ever before. Now that we know who our main characters are, we can begin the process of moving closer one day at a time...

Awesome Blast

# Notes

1. Mishnah Rosh Hashanah 1:2, Talmud Rosh Hashanah 8:1-17, Isaiah 33:22.
2. Exodus 19:5, Deuteronomy 7:6, Deuteronomy 33:3, Jeremiah 31:3,
3. Following suit with the idea of "the King is in the Field." Rabbi Shneur Zalman of Liadi, the Alter Rebbe, the founding spiritual leader of Chabad, explained the reason for this special closeness during the month of Elul "is comparable to a king who returns to the city, and when he passes through the fields on his way to the palace, anyone who wishes may get close and greet him as he passes through the fields. This is important, because once he is in his palace, entry is only possible to those with special permission. So too, during the month of Elul, all go out into the field to greet the King as he passes through."
4. A major theme of the Rosh HaShanah liturgy is our crowning God as King. The opening tefillah of the Rosh HaShanah Shacharit begins with a simple term of *HaMelech*—המלך (the King).
5. The final prayer service of Yom Kippur is called *Neilah*, which literally means locked in. The concept is that we are finally having a private audience with God, and it is just each one of us and God alone. This mirrors the process that many Jewish couples have of locking themselves into a private room alone after the *Chuppah*, in order to seal the deal that they are officially a married couple.
6. Exodus 34:6—7.
7. Song of Songs 6:3.

# The Energies of the Month of Elul[1]

**Sense:** Action—The sense of the month is action. Taking action. Morah Leah Golomb explains that, "Every year for every person has a different purpose. If you are still here, it's because there is something you are supposed to be doing." Is there some action you wish to take in your life?

**Tribe:** Gad—The tribe of Gad was known to be good at organizing. Do you feel called to organize any particular part of your life before the New Year? Sort out any personal business?

**Body Part:** The left hand. The left hand is connected to the heart. If you were to tune into your heart regarding how you want to live this upcoming year, what might you hear it saying?

Elul also has the **numerological value** of 67, which is *Bina*, implying a deep heart-felt understanding. If you could offer yourself a heart-felt-Oscar-award-winning display of understanding right now, what would it literally sound like? (That is an invitation to express it to yourself outloud.)

# Awesome Blast

**Letter:** The letter *Yud*. The *yud* represents the point. We can ask ourselves, "What is the point of my life? What is my mission? What am I doing here? What is my 'why'?"

*Yud* is the only letter that floats, that is beyond nature. It hints at our ability to rise above. It shows that we can rise above the resentments. Are there any resentments you wish to look at or work through in honor of the New Year?

**Astrological Sign / Mazal**—Virgo, the Virgin, the *Betulah*. The Sfat Emet reminds us from the Song of Songs, that inside each one of us is an untouched place, like a sealed spring in a locked garden, a *'maayan chatum began na'ul.'*[2] The idea? No matter how we may have messed up this year, there is something within us that remains pure that we can tap back into.

Another way of looking at the concept of virginity is of someone that is ready to come close. Can we find that in ourselves? To whom or what might we be seeking closeness? And as my EFT teacher Pearl Lopian says, 'what if anger is really just, I am so upset that we aren't connected?'

**Planet:** Kochav כוכב, or Mercury. Kaf & Vav (כו 26 =) and Kaf & Bet (22=כב). 26 is the numerical value of God's Y-K-V-K name. 22 is the amount of letters of the Hebrew Alphabet. Together they illustrate the power of the planet and the month, which is communication. We learn to communicate properly with each other by bringing Godliness (26) into our speech (22). This month invites us into the bravery to communicate honestly and vulnerably. Is there anyone with whom you would like to practice conscious communication?

**Rosh Chodesh Elul in History:** At the conclusion of the second forty day and forty night period (that is, on the 29th of Av, Erev Rosh Chodesh Elul), G-d forgave the Jewish People and instructed Moshe to ascend Har Sinai yet again the next day, to receive the Second Luchos, on which would be inscribed for the second time the Ten Commandments. Can you imagine the strength, the faith, the bravery and the fortitude to go back up and try again on behalf of the people? Is there anything in your life that is beckoning you to try again?

## Epic tidbits about the Month of Elul according to two of my super-dope Teachers:

*Morah Leah Golomb~*

- Elul is really the end of the year. And at the end of the year, we're all a little bit broken, like the *luchot*.[3] You aren't alone. Deep breaths. What if brokenness and contraction were just the polarities of wholeness and expansion?

- Hashem tells Moses to fashion new tablets, like the first ones. In other words, it doesn't matter how far gone we are. The headquarters of the month of Elul is Moshe returning up to Har Sinai to try again. After they had a

## Awesome Blast

drunken orgy[4] and literally did all three of the biggest *aveirot*, sins: murder, idolatry, and sexual misconduct... if they could be forgiven and start again, so can we. There is no despair. What if you trusted that it is going to be okay, and chose to relax and enjoy the unfolding?

*Reb' David Sacks~*

- Rosh Chodesh Elul marks the beginning of a period of 40 days of forgiving and self examination that ends at the closing prayer (*Neila*) on Yom Kippur. Elul is likened to 'a *mikvah*[5] in time'[6] because there are 40 days until Yom Kippur, and there are 40 *se'ah*[7] of water in a kosher mikvah. There are also 24 hours in a day and 24 *logim*[8] in each *se'ah*, so the *mikvah* metaphor really parallels the time period. He explains that the month of Elul, like the *mikvah*, is the deepest cleanser. What do you want to be cleansed of?

   But there is one caveat! The laws of going to the *mikvah* involve going in free of clothes/ anything connected to our physical bodies. The Rabbis explain that you can't go into a *mikvah* holding a *sheretz*, or a creepy-crawly sort of animal/bug/rodent. *Shratzim* are typically nonkosher creatures, and this idea hints to the fact that you can't hold onto unkosher/impure ideas/thoughts while attempting to purify yourself. So if Elul is a *mikvah* in time, what idea/s might you want to let go of so you can come out renewed and pure?

- Reb David also explains that the Talmud teaches that Hashem created *tshuva* before He created the world.[9] And everything is a fractal. So it's like now in Elul, before He creates the world again, he has to bring down the powers, the *kochot*, of *tshuva* again. And, because *tshuva* was created before the world, it is not subject to the natural order of the world, and that is why *tshuva* goes beyond our *mazal*. What would you love for your path of *tshuva* to allow for, assuming anything was possible?

# Notes

1. According to the mystical book the *Sefer Yetzirah*, every month is connected to a sense, one of the 12 Tribes of Israel, a body part, a Hebrew letter, an astrological sign, a planet, a permutation of God's name and more. Here I am providing just a few of the connections to the month to help orient the reader towards what energies are available during the month and worth holding consciousness around for enhanced spiritual awareness.
2. Song of Songs 4:12.
3. The *"luchot"* referred to here are the tablets that had the 10 commandments written on them that Moses smashed when he saw the worship of the Golden Calf.
4. The commentaries about the Golden Calf point to drunkenness and extreme sexual misconduct
5. A mikvah is a ritual bath used for cleansing spiritual impurity and restoring us to our original state of purity.
6. The Bnei Yissaschar is a classic Chassidic text, written by Rabbi Zvi Elimelech Shapiro of Dinov.
7. A *se'ah* is a Biblical measurement.
8. A *log* is another Biblical measurement, *logim* is the plural.
9. Netivot Shalom p. 106., Breishit Rabbah 1:4.

# The Power of Renewal

**Av 30**

*Rosh Chodesh Elul*

Rosh Chodesh Elul is a two-day celebration[1] that begins on the last day of Av. The tradition of hearing the Shofar in Elul typically begins on the 1st of Elul[2] itself rather than on the last day of Av.[3] *And,* I am a bit of a renegade and I don't wish to wait even another day, so I love to start playing Shofar today! Hearing the Shofar every day in Elul is a sacred tradition but not a Jewish law, so it is not *halachically* problematic to start a day early.[4]

But wait, why is the New Year two days? *Can you imagine the ball dropping two nights in a row in Times Square? AWKWARD.*

Rabbi Shlomo Carlebach explains that we start the year with the knowledge that *there is always a second chance.*

Newness, or *hitchadshut*, is the name of the game in Judaism. Rosh Hashanah strangely being two days is just the seed of bringing this idea of second chances into the year. This message is even imparted within the name of the holiday itself. *Rosh* means 'head', and *Hashana*, technically means 'of the year', as in 'head of the year.' But *Hashana* also shares the root of the word *leshanot*, which means to change. In other words Rosh Hashana can

*Shofar in Tulum, Mexico*

mean 'the head of the year,' but it can also imply 'to change your mindset,' or *'leshanot et harosh.'*

*And* because Rosh Hashanah is also the celebration of the new month, it also contains the energy of a *Rosh Chodesh*. What is that? *Rosh*, as we said means 'head', and *Chodesh*, technically means 'month', as in 'head of the month.' But *Chodesh* also shares the root of the word *chadash*, which means new. In other words, Rosh Chodesh can mean 'the head of the month,' but it can also imply 'a new mindset,' or *'rosh chadash.'*

This *hitchadshut*, or energy of renewal, is imperative for any authentic spiritual path, because the knowledge that you can always begin again is the counterforce to the world's greatest liar, the voice of despair.[5] God never gives up on us, so why should we? The religious Jewish world has an expression for someone who 'left the religious path,' and that is that 'they fell off the wagon.' But Reb David Sacks politely laughs at this idea by saying that they just fell onto another wagon! All wagons, and all paths lead us back to God. And if that is the case, there is always a second chance in this life-long soul journey. But when and where did this whole journey of mankind begin?

# Awesome Blast

## Notes

1. Even though the Torah in Vayikra 23:24 ordains only one day, Talmud Yerushalmi Eruvin 3:9 and Rambam in Hilchot Kiddush ha-Chodesh 5:7-8 explain that Rosh Hashanah was established as 2 days by the early prophets to cover for technical issues that may occur due to the fact that the new moon was based on the testimony of witnesses, and so this would essentially 'cover the bases' and make sure we would celebrate the New Year on the correct day. Today the 2 days are often referred to as one long day, but with certain practical implications in *halacha*.
2. The Magen Avrohom (581:2).
3. In Pirkei d'Rabi Eliezer, Perek 46, Chazal say that a shofar was blown on Rosh Chodesh Elul when Moshe Rabbeinu went up to Mount Sinai for the final 40 days. This is the source for blowing shofar during the month of Elul.
4. Kovetz Halachos (Yomim Noraim 1:19).
5. Rebbe Nachman says there is no such thing as despair in the world, at all. Likutei Moharan, Part II 78:7:3.

# The Very First Shofar

We have a Kabbalistic tradition about the first Shofar. It was actually the (unified) body of Adam-Eve! What? Were Adam and Eve harmonizing in the Garden or something and it sounded like Shofar calls?

Actually, we learn that when God blew the breath of life into Adam-Eve,[1] it made a sound, and that sound was the original Shofar.[2]

*WAIT THAT IS MINDBLOWING, SAY THAT AGAIN! When God blew the breath of life into Adam-Eve, it made a sound, and that sound was the original Shofar?!*

We, our bodies, when infused with the breath of God/Life actually make this holy resonant sound! Or another way of saying it is that then and now, we come alive through the sound of the Shofar. *Wow.*

It is definitely an esoteric concept, but also super cool to explore. It is not so far from what New Age folk are often quoted to say, that we were created by sound. According to the first chapter in Genesis, God created the whole world with ten spoken utterances.[3] So yes, we, and all of Creation were essentially created by sound. And this Kabbalistic explanation about God blowing

Shofar at Kenneth Hahn Park

## Awesome Blast

breath into the unified Adam-Eve body adds that we, *ourselves*, the body, was not only created with sound, but also became the first Shofar.

So the very first Shofar was the first human? *Yup!* But before God blew this first breath of life into the body of man, He had to have made the physical body of man, right? *Yup!* How did He make man? Did He do that with sound too? Let's work backwards a little bit.

The verse says that the body was formed from the dust of the Earth. "And the Lord God formed man of the dust of the ground, and breathed into his nostrils the breath of life; and man became a living soul."[4] We know that that name for man, or Adam, comes from the word *adamah*, or earth. *But what earth?* Which handful of earth did God choose to create the first human? The earth from Machu Picchu? The Maldives? The Hawaiian Islands?

Rashi[5] draws our attention to the origin of the earth from which Adam was formed. In one opinion he suggests that God gathered dust from the four corners of the world. In a second opinion, Rashi points out[6] that Adam was created from the dust beneath the altar (the *mizbe'ach*) of the site of the future Temple. The altar is where people would come to offer sacrifices in order to spiritually show up and own up, to request forgiveness, and to offer thanks. In other words, the first man was literally created from the place of *tshuva*. What does this mean? It means that you and I are literally created from the place of *our tshuva*. We become our truest selves when we are willing to show up, own up, apologize, ask forgiveness, and vulnerably offer thanks. *Wow. So deep.*

So physically, we are created from the place of our *tshuva*, and spiritually, we are infused with life through the breath of God, and together, this creates the call that was and is the sound of the Shofar. Our collective resonance with the Shofar call and its call to *tshuva* is literally in our physical and spiritual genes!

Now, let's take it one step further. Even though you and I didn't personally experience that first breath of God vibrating through our bodies, we can still experience *each* breath we receive as a gift of life-force from God.[7]

*UM SHEESH* that sounds intimidating to receive *every* breath as if God is giving us our life-force anew. Perhaps we can try receiving our very next conscious breath as if it was the one that first gave man life? How about try riiiight now?

*By the way, Nili, why do you keep writing 'receive' a breath, as opposed to 'take a breath'? Well friends, get ready for a mic drop...*

*We can never 'take' a breath. We can ONLY 'receive' a breath, from the One giving it to us. WHOAAA! Stay tuned... it's about to get even deeper and more intimate!*

Awesome Blast

# Notes

1. (Genesis 2:7) "The LORD God formed Adam of dust from the ground and breathed into his nostrils the breath of life, and Adam became a living creature", & Ramban wrote, "The One who blew, blew some of his own essence". For further reading check out "Breath of Life" an online article by Rabbi Shlomo Schachter.
2. Shem MiShmuel quoting Avnei Nezer, Gemara Rosh Hashanah 15:7.
3. Genesis 1 & Ethics of Our Fathers, Pirkei Avot 5:1.
4. Genesis 2:7.
5. One of the most famous Torah commentators.
6. Shemot 20:21.
7. Rebbe Nachman of Breslov teaches that with each breath, every moment, we are given the opportunity to connect anew to our life's source and to our soul. Also see Talmud Brachot 58b on sighing.

# The Intimate Bond, The French Kiss, & the Magen David

**Elul 1**

*Also Rosh Chodesh Elul*

I had an epic *chiddush* (new idea)! The sages say that God gives us the Torah as a gift to us,[1] and then we give back God our *tfilah* (our prayer) as our gift to Him.[2] Reciprocity. So perhaps in a similar vein, God breathed life into us as a gift, and so we take that Shofar on Elul and the holidays—the vessel through which God gave us life and expression[3]—and blow our *own* life force, our own breath, back to Him as our return gift.

*The truth is it sounds a whole lot like the intimate exchange that is a French Kiss! What is a French Kiss if not the intimate exchange of breath! WHOA AGAIN.*

Perhaps this is one of the reasons the Shofar call is often so moving. It is like the return call of a lover to her Beloved. We already know that Elul is famously an acronym in Hebrew for 'I am for my Beloved and my Beloved is for me.'[4] But when you phrase it like an exchange of life-force and a French Kiss it just becomes a

Shofar in Zion National Park

## Awesome Blast

lot more feel-able. Come backkk, I misssss you, I want you close... closer... closer!

And maybe it's that very reciprocation which creates an intimate bond, solidifying our love so we can then have a baby called the New Year!

In fact, we also see this bond in the symbol which represents our whole tradition: the *Magen David*! The Jewish star, translated as the shield or the protector of David has a triangle pointing down, representing God's coming down to us and a triangle pointing up, representing our reaching back up to God.[5] This reciprocation creates a union. And it is the very union of the two giving to each other which protects us. The in-tact relationship *is* our protection. So perhaps it is the reciprocation of our breath back through the Shofar which creates the intimate bond between us and God, that keeps us safe and well!

## Notes

1. Ethics of Our Fathers, Pirkei Avot 1:1, Talmud Nedarim 38, Talmud Eiruvin 54a.
2. Bilvavi Mishkan Evne, The teachings of Rebbe Nachman.
3. Genesis 2:7.
4. Song of Songs 6:3.
5. The Zohar (3:73a).

# Mindfulness & a Spiritual Accounting of the Soul

*Elul*
**2**

The simple reason we are highlighting the Shofar tradition for the month of Elul as opposed to the next month of Tishrei when the high holidays actually begin, is because there is a tradition to hear the Shofar every day in Elul[1] (except Shabbat) leading up to Rosh Hashanah. It is truly an ancient exercise in mindfulness.

Hearing the shofar every day in Elul reminds us that it is time to prepare for the great spiritual energy that is available to us on Rosh Hashanah and throughout the High Holidays. Rosh Hashanah is not just the New Year, but the seed of the New Year. *Or as Reb Shlomo Carlebach puts it, it is the headquarters of the year!* Whatever we put into that seed can then grow and blossom in the year ahead.[2] What we sow, we shall reap, bH.

*So Nili, you are telling me that hearing or blowing the Shofar every day is a mindfulness practice to help us realize a new portal for growth is opening, but what the heck am I supposed to do to get from mindfulness to behavioral changes?[3]*

Shofar in Utah

### Awesome Blast

Mindfulness that a new spiritual growth opportunity is upon us IS the first step. But to go from mindfulness to behavioral changes, we need process. And we can learn that process from God Himself!

A spiritual accounting happens on Rosh Hashanah. What exactly is this spiritual accounting?[4] A spiritual accounting is like an IRS audit but way less scary and way more loving. God calls an executive meeting with each of us on the New Year and asks, *'yo homie, how you been doing?'* And it is up to us to have really contemplated the answer during the month leading up to that 'meeting' and to come prepared with insights into ourselves.

So the daily Shofar blasts in the month of Elul remind us that it is the time to be mindful of taking a soul-accounting[5] (in Hebrew this is called a *Cheshbon HaNefesh*) and invite consciousness around our thoughts, speech, and actions from the past year, and around how we want to walk through the world during the year ahead.

*It's like an OG Jewish consciousness practice. (OG means Original Gangsta.) Cuz the real gangsta-flex is showing up for yourself.*

And let's get real. If you wait til the night before, chances are you won't truly have expanded your consciousness, nor have time to really take account of your actions. So yes, mindfulness and accounting begin now.

# Elul 2

## *DROP EVERYTHING AND REFER TO THE MOST VALUABLE PART OF THIS BOOK*
### *on page 182*
### *Nili's Famous Fun Practical Guide to Doing Basic Tshuva!*

*Why drop everything now? You are at the start of Elul. If you begin the work now, you have a realistic chance of some REALLY AWESOME SOUL ACCOUNTING—*
### *YOU GOT THIS!!!*

## Notes

1. The earliest source for this is Pirkei d'Rabbi Eliezer (46), where the custom is mentioned only regarding the first of Elul.
2. A beautiful teaching that I learned from Morah Leah Golomb from Reb Shlomo Carlebach is, what makes one apple more delicious than another apple? The prayer of the seed.
3. Mindfulness & Behavioral Changes, Harvard Rev Psychiatry. 2020 Nov 6;28(6):371—394.
4. See the teachings of Rabbi Israel Salanter, Rebbe Nachman, of Rabbi Yosef Yitzchak Schneersohn, the sixth Lubavitcher Rebbe, and Rabbi Menachem Mendel Leffin's book Cheshbon HaNefesh, an early 19th-century guide to introspection and self-improvement.
5. Amos 3:6.

# Manifestation, the Messiah & Limiting Beliefs

## Elul 3

One of the most important 'rules' in manifestation is to notice any limiting beliefs. You can't manifest something if you don't believe it is possible. What is a belief in the first place? Abraham Hicks explains that *a belief is just a thought that you keep thinking*. One of the incredible inherent messages of the Shofar is hope and the idea that everything is possible... if you believe it, you can receive it!

And, the sages teach us that we can only receive what we *believe* we can receive. Why?

*The Shofar will be blown and heard all over the world to announce the coming of the Messiah.*[1] What does the Messiah have to do with hope? The Messianic Era is the time during which there will be peace in our hearts, world peace, total healing, love, understanding and joy![2] Basically, anything you dream of manifesting will surely unfold for the good during that time. So hearing the Shofar is actually a reminder that we are collectively manifesting this Great Day and this Great Era, and that there is hope for not only the whole world, but also for you! You can't have a redeemed world without every

Shofar in Bryce National Park

single person in it being redeemed as well. To help clarify the 'Biblical-speak' of what it means to be 'redeemed,' it simply means to be emotionally freed from all mental and physical slavery and constrictions. And of course for this to be possible, no limiting beliefs can apply.

But wait, what is a limiting belief? A limiting belief is a thought or state of mind that you think is the absolute truth and stops you from doing certain things. Sometimes we are aware that we have these beliefs, and sometimes we have to dig a little to expose these beliefs. They don't always have to be about yourself, either. They could be about how the world works, ideas, and how you interact with people.

Some examples of limiting beliefs are: I'm not smart enough to lead this meeting. I don't have enough experience for this big career move. I'll never be successful. I don't have enough money to enjoy my life. No one will ever love me. I don't sing. I can't wear that, it's not in my character. I could never teach.

Limiting beliefs can also be in terms of believing that you even have the courage to try on a new belief system. But here's the cool thing: we call the *Mashiach, Mashiach ben Partzi*.[3] Technically this means that the Messiah will be from the lineage of a man named Peretz,[4] the son of Tamar, and the ancestor of King David.[5] But nothing is random in Judaism, and Hebrew words carry deep meanings. Peretz, and Partzi share the root of the word *poretz*, which means to break through. What does this mean about the energy of the Messiah? Of redemption? It means that redemption, both nationally and personally, only comes as the result of some form of breakthrough. In general, if nothing is broken through, things remain the same. In other words, if nothing changes, nothing changes. If we wish for great change and transformation, we MUST break through our current ways of believing and behaving. So yes, it might be scary to try a different thought than you have ever tried or to believe everything is possible for you. It might be nerve-wracking to get ready to shine brighter, but you might just want to try... to feel the fear and do it anyway.[6]

You already have a no, you may as well try a yes! The sky isn't even the limit. God is called 'Hakol Yechol,' or the One for Whom everything is possible... and good news, this Unlimited Force is what your very soul is made of...[7] *yallah*, let's get this limitless party started!

## Notes

1. Isaiah 27:13.

2. Isaiah 9:3-4.

3. You might recognize this from the *Lecha Dodi* prayer written by Rav Shlomo Alkebetz in the *Kabbalat Shabbat* service. It calls the *Mashiach* "*Ish ben Parzti*," a man, son of Parzti.

4. Genesis 38:27-30.

5. Ruth 4:18.

6. Of course while respecting your own boundaries and inner voice! The bravery must be in integrity with self-respect for healthy change!

7. Our souls are described in the Tanya Chapter 2, based on Job, as a "chelek Eloka mi'ma'al mamish," or a literal piece of God, an actual part of God Himself.

# Sound Healing & Frequencies

*Elul*
**4**

Sound baths, crystal sound bowls, gongs, frequency-music, and talking about resonance are all so popular these days! As Nikola Tesla said, "If you want to find the secrets of the universe, think in terms of energy, frequency and vibration."

Nili, you're telling me that sound can help heal? Explain.

First, I recommend going to a sound bath so you can feel it for yourself. It's legit…don't knock it til' you try it. The experience of a good sound bath can bring people to great calm and/or to tremendous irritation and subsequent excavation of suppressed emotion. But the truth is, you don't need to go to a sound bath to understand the power of sound. You know the experience of standing in synagogue on Rosh Hashanah… It's usually boring, boring, boring, and then *you hear that Shofar, it shakes you, and you can feel the resonance, you can feel its power. It truly is an awesome blast.*[1]

I would like to share an idea about resonance that helped me really understand it. Imagine I had perfect pitch and I sang an A note. So I start singing this A note, and meanwhile there is a tuned guitar leaning on the wall on the other side of the room. A guitar has an A string. *So if*

Shofar at Red Rocks Canyon

## Awesome Blast

*you had a microscope and put it over the A string, you would see that the string would be microscopically vibrating! Why? Because of the resonance.[2]*

*In the world of psychotherapy, this also explains why we get triggered.[3] There is spiritual resonance.*

What is happening spiritually when there is resonance? There are two ways to understand resonance. One is when it hits you on the same note like the metaphor of the guitar string. In a personal example, I have found myself triggered by any given woman who walks in the room all loud and confident. I might find her annoying or just feel repulsed by her. Once I become conscious of what is going on with my emotional reaction, I can have a good laugh at my response because the truth is, I AM the loud confident woman who walks into a room. And when I am triggered by another like myself, it can bring up all sorts of subconscious fears about how people might experience me in unpleasant ways, or how I might not actually love the qualities that accompany being loud and confident. I might have thought judgmentally about her, 'can't she see we're in a conversation?,' or 'wow she only thinks about herself,' or 'what a bulldozer,' but the truth is the trigger relieves when I realize that those are my very behaviors and potential effect on others and I am uncomfortable seeing it!

Now there is also the inverse experience of resonance. It is when someone or something resonates or triggers you, but in no way similar to the way one experiences themselves. In a personal example, I once found myself perpetually triggered by a good friend of mine. And as a student of consciousness, I would often reflect and wonder what it was that was bothering me so much. I couldn't figure it out! I judged her as selfish, immodest and irresponsible. But of all of my poor qualities, I really did not identify with these three. If anything I used to overgive, overdress, and was overly responsible, to a fault. And then it became clear to me what was really going on… and the discovery changed my life. What was happening emotionally?

I was so triggered at these behaviors because I WOULD NEVER LET MYSELF behave in those ways. And it is not that I *wanted* to be selfish, immodest or irresponsible, but watching someone else give themselves full permission to do and be those things triggered my discomfort with my own severity, strictness, and personal limits on unconditional self-love. In effect what it was showing me is where I would not love myself unconditionally—if I portrayed any hint of those qualities, I was (subconsciously) not willing to accept myself. I was not allowing myself any space or room for those qualities and so my emotional triggers went ballistic when I encountered her. But we are all really just encountering ourselves in every interaction. And now? Now I love this woman sans triggers and have given myself way more permission to be human. Can you relate?

Now that we really get emotional resonance, let's bring it back to physical resonance and the Shofar. What is happening scientifically when there is physical resonance? Certain sound frequencies stimulate the body's natural healing mechanisms. When we are exposed to sound, our brain waves entrain to the frequency of the sound, and frequencies are believed to be correlated with emotions up the emotional scale.[4] The lowest of frequencies correlates with shame, and as the frequency rises it corresponds

## Awesome Blast

with guilt, apathy, grief, fear, desire, anger, pride, courage, neutrality, willingness, acceptance, reason, love, peace, joy and excitement. While I have not found any studies on the sound healing effects on the shofar, I find it quite fascinating to ponder what is happening to the vibration of our cells as the Shofar sounds.

When researching how the Shofar is made I came across this interview with Shofar maker Maurice Kamins. He reported, "'as I'm sanding them, there's a moment when the horn itself will start vibrating with the tone it will give once the horn is blown," he says with reverence. First I thought this was just super cool in and of itself, and I took this as a metaphor for our spiritual work. Sometimes, as we are being refined, we can catch glimpses of how we will look and feel on the other side of a healing process and that inspires us to continue our work. Wow!

## Notes

1. If you, the reader, have never had this experience, or have not attended synagogues, reach out to your local Jewish community and give it a try!
2. Further explained in TDK Corporations Tech-Mag article, The Wonders of Electromagnetism. What is Resonance Phenomenon? Mechanism of tuning circuits.
3. Further explained in University of Northern Carolina's article, Understanding Mental Health Triggers.
4. Brittney-Nichole Connor-Savarda explains in her article, The Science Behind Emotional Energy: Exploring the Vibrations of Our Emotional World, "A groundbreaking study by Dr. David R. Hawkins and the Institute of Noetic Sciences demonstrated the existence of an energy field generated by various emotions, sometimes described as a "consciousness field." Using a technique called Applied Kinesiology, Dr. Hawkins developed a scale that assigned distinct frequency values to different emotions, ranging from shame (20) to enlightenment (700+). Emotions such as fear and anger had lower frequencies, while emotions like love and joy were found to have higher frequencies.

   Based on these findings, researchers have also delved into the therapeutic potential of using emotional energy in healing practices. Dr. William Tiller, a former Stanford University professor, found that positive emotional states could aid the healing process. This research has further led to the development of healing modalities like Reiki and the Emotional Freedom Technique (EFT), which manipulate emotional energy fields to improve well-being.

# Listening & Intuition: The Keys to Personal Peace, Peace in the Home, and Peace in the World

**Elul 5**

I can't help but chuckle that the central *mitzvah* that we are discussing—listening to the Shofar—is commanded to the most stereotypically talkative culture on earth! Why is that so funny? All we do is talk, and the *mitzvah* is to listen! The *mitzvah* is actually just to listen. Can you even imagine a version of the 90's TV show, the Nanny, where she just deeply listened?

On one hand, it could seem obvious that the call to hear the Shofar is a call to listen,[1] *like duh,* but on the other hand, whooaaaaa, how trippy... the call of the Shofar is a call to listen???!!!

It's as if God is hinting at us in a not-so-subtle way that perhaps the way to *tshuva* and self-refinement begins with listening.

*But why would listening to the Shofar specifically help a person refine themselves?*

Shofar in the Caribbean Sea

Elul 5

Some sages say that the sound of the Shofar is the sound of your own soul!

Some sages say that the sound of the Shofar is the voice of God!

Hearing the sound of one's soul or the voice of God Himself could certainly be clarifying and guide us onto elevated paths.

An interesting intention for listening to the Shofar is asking yourself, *if this was the voice of my soul calling, what would it be saying? Or, if this was the voice of God speaking to me, what might I hear Him saying?*

*Pro-tip: Don't just ask yourself these questions as you read this, but try it out! Open up a Shofar video to listen for the answers. Just as you can practice yoga or practice piano, we can also actually practice listening.*

Not only does listening help us tune into the voice of our soul and the voice of God, but it also allows us to emulate God. *Why?* I learned from my teacher Morah Leah Golomb that God is called *HaMakom*, which means 'The Place,' because He makes a place and a space for all of us in His world. So too, when we make a space for others in our own world, especially by listening to another, we emulate God. *So sweet.*

Ok, so *tshuva* begins with listening to the call of your own soul, listening to the call of God, and returning to our Godly essence of making space. But what even is the call of your own soul? Loosely translated, the call of your soul can be thought of as your intuition, or your will. Developing the abilities to both listen to your intuition and then follow it seems to be the key to joyful living. In fact, one of the most important life-hacks that I have learned is that following my intuition.

## Awesome Blast

Even when—or perhaps especially when—it is NOT logical, it guides me well and keeps me in flow. For example, logic says, 'the party happening tonight is supposed to be so fun. All of my friends are going. Something like this probably won't happen again any time soon. And it's right around the block from me.' But my intuition says, 'no thank you, I don't want to go.' Or, you are about to leave your house and you hear a voice that says, 'hey take a Band Aid™ with you.' Why? Who knows? But later when you hear someone ask for a Band Aid™, it all makes sense. It doesn't matter if your intuition is the most illogical thing in the world. Ignoring or not listening to one's intuition will often lead to less smooth or even challenging experiences. *You feel me? You know that moment when you felt, 'I knew I should have/shouldn't have... and I didn't listen to my intuition! Shoot!'*

Living in alignment feels like flow, feels like ease, feels like harmony. Living out of alignment feels like struggle, going against the current, feels like discomfort, feels like misery. Why can it feel so uncomfortable? Because it's God's most gracious guidance system. God is trying to let us know that we are off track and need to listen, reassess, and redirect. Our emotional experience can help us tell whether or not we are in alignment with ourselves and God. Listening in, feeling in, tuning in to the call. How else can we grow and refine ourselves if we don't listen in? And that is all included in the simple powerful message of the *mitzvah* of the Shofar... listen!

But why is listening to our intuition specifically a Jewish idea? Here is the spiritual science: We have what is called '*ratzon*'. "The Kabbalists explain that *ratzon*, will or desire, is the most powerful force within the human being."[2] Rabbi

Mordechai Elazar Koenig explains that "Reb Noson says that it is impossible to describe in writing the greatness of our *ratzon* and yearning to do the Will of G-d." He explains that the entire reason the soul is compelled to descend from the Upper Worlds into this physical world is only for the sake of *ratzon*."[3] Here we meet the intersection between Kabbalah and New Age spirituality.

You know that popular word, "alignment"? The reason that *ratzon* is so important is because there is a 'lower'[4] *ratzon*, our intuition/will/desire, and then there is a 'higher' *Ratzon*, which is God's. Kabbalistically speaking, our 'lower' personal divine *ratzon* channels down through the Tree of Life, the spiritual energy channels through which the world is created, from the highest point of *Keter*, which is 'higher *Ratzon*,' or God's Will! In other words, when we tune into and listen to our divine *ratzon*, to our intuition, we are getting into alignment with God's Will for us and the world.[5] *In other words, the true voice of your soul is an expression of the voice of God, channeling through you to guide you through life!*

But how do we decipher if the inner voice is leading us in the ways of goodness or if it is a deceitful voice? This is an ongoing process of the work of listening, but one tip is to see if the voices that speak to you in your mind are kind or cruel. Reb David Sacks explains that a Godly voice will speak to you kindly.[6] Practically speaking, one can also learn to practice muscle testing to train oneself in really listening to one's intuition. If the term 'muscle-testing' is new to you, please go check it out! It's a freakin' epic practice of listening to and through the body itself.

## Awesome Blast

When do you, Nili, listen to your intuition? I try to listen in for nearly every decision I make. From what to eat, to what to wear, to which cafe to choose in order to work on this very book, to deciding when to stay in any given place and when to go, I listen in. Why? I feel that that is how I can follow God's guidance and be most aligned with His Will for greatest Divine Providence, success, ease, joy and personal peace.

Is this message of listening to the voice of our soul reflected elsewhere in the Jewish tradition? The simple answer might shock you. Listening isn't just some Kabbalistic and New Age Shofar phenomenon, it is actually the central tenet of our faith! Did you catch it yet? Some of us may have missed the memo even while reciting it every day since childhood!

THE central tenet of our faith is "*SHEMA Yisrael Hashem Elokeinu Hashem Echad!*"[7] *Shema*, Listen! So in the *Shema*, we are meant to listen. But to what?

Let us look at the first part of the sentence, "*Hashem Elokeinu.*" We are meant to listen up and understand that "God is our God."

What does it mean that "God is our God?" It means that the One Who is running the world is also running the circumstances of our lives, and speaking to us through them! That God is guiding us! If we listen, we can learn so much from the patterns, messages and signs that God gives us so generously.

I learned through Shadow Work that any time we see something come up in our lives even twice, it is already considered a pattern, and therefore something to pay attention to. You got stolen from twice in one month? Pay attention. People keep offering you the same unique compliment in one week? Pay attention, God is our God. He is with us in every moment, in every circumstance, in every place, and in every person we interact with. The more we listen, the more we can learn and grow. This idea that God is our God and is active in every aspect of our lives runs in perfect parallel with the idea above that listening to our own *ratzon* will then connect us into God's *Ratzon*.

*And guess what, it gets better.* Once we truly begin to listen, not only can we align ourselves with Divine guidance and have greater personal peace, but we can then have greater peace with others as well.

*Now you gotta hear what happened as I was writing this section on listening. I had woken up with the question, where should I work today? I asked my soul, listened in, and got an answer for a specific cafe on the beach that I had never been to. I sat down to work and I was surprised to see my brotha' Rav Pesach Stadlin—who lives in another city—walking up to me to say hi. He asked what I was working on, and then said, 'by the way, listening is also the key to Shalom Bayit and to peace in the world!', just as I was about to write about it... How's that for alignment?! So here is what he had to share...*

He said that *Shalom Bayit*, both international and 'inter-home-ular,' comes from the ability to listen to a perspective beyond our own. We often take our own narrative and put it so close to our ears, that that is all we can hear. And one of the keys to *Shalom Bayit*, both little *bayit* (one's own home) and big *bayit* (the world) is to hear more, to cultivate the art of compassionate listening, and to hold the others' narratives alongside our own. Once you can hold the others' perspective and properly articulate it, usually peacemaking is *chick-chack* after that! *To that I say AMEN brotha!*

And in complete flow, it came to no surprise that one of my favorite songs that Rav Pesach often plays on his guitar for our friends is sung to the Chinese Proverb;

"If there is light in the soul,

There will be beauty in the person.

If there is beauty in the person,

There will be harmony in the house.

If there is harmony in the house,

There will be order in the nation.

If there is order in the nation,

There will be peace on Earth...."

The key is listening. And every year, when people around the world practice listening to the Shofar every day for a month in order to prepare ourselves to deeply listen to the Shofar on Rosh Hashanah, we begin the year with a most powerful practice of listening that can teach us how to have greater personal peace, peace in the home, and peace in the world.

## Notes

1. Rambam, Hilkhot Shofar 3:10.
2. Menachem Feldman from Hayom Yom, Elul 18, based on the teachings of the Baal Shem Tov.
3. Based on Likutei Halachot, Arev, Halacha 3.
4. Lower and higher here are not to imply less and more than, but rather, connected to earthly realms versus connected to heavenly realms.
5. Kabbalistically speaking, we have aligned the *sfira* of *Malchut* with the sfira of *Keter*.
6. Reb David shared this based on a teaching that says that when God asks Avraham to undertake the most difficult test of bringing Yitzchak to sacrifice, He uses the Hebrew word, *'na'* which means please. In other words, if it is a Godly voice, and a Godly intuition, it will have an element of kindness, or at least neutrality, but not cruelty or harshness.
7. "Hear, O Israel, the L-rd is our G-d, the L-rd is One." Deuteronomy 6:4—9, 11:13—21; Numbers 15:37—41.

# Self Improvement, Self-Respect, the Patriarchs & a Mind-blowing Definition of Tshuva

**Elul 6**

So if you have been following the daily videos and teachings, you have already caught on to the fact that the Shofar is a call to aspire to our highest self in the upcoming year. It is a call to healing, growth, consciousness and change. Somehow the secrets of self-improvement do seem to be found in sound!

In fact the word "Shofar" shares the root of the Hebrew word "*leShaPeR*," or, to improve.[1] Self reflexively, the word "*lehiSHtaPeR*," connotes improving oneself. *What?! No way! That's deep.*

Now that is cool enough in and of itself, but are there any hidden secrets as to how to improve ourselves within the Shofar service? There are!

Kabbalistically,[2] each of the calls of the Shofar, the *tekia*, *shevarim*, and *truah* represent the patriarchs: Avraham (Abraham), Yitzchak (Isaac) and Yaakov (Jacob). Avraham represents divine loving-kindness, Isaac represents divine strength/boundaries, and Yaakov represents

Shofar in the Court of the Patriarchs, Zion

## Elul 6

divine mercy. Why does this give us insight into how to improve ourselves? Well, it is all about navigating our *middot*, character traits, and noticing if we are living in balance.

Living in balance requires paying attention to how we employ each *middah*. For example, let us look at Avraham's quality of kindness. If I am being extremely kind to everyone around me, doing favors for people, and really extending myself to help others, I might be simultaneously way out of balance with kindness towards myself or my own family. I may have given all of my time and attention to others while denying myself the time and attention I need to be well and happy. An imbalance in kindness towards others can lead to resentment, as neglect of our own needs almost always results in subconscious bitterness.

And if the imbalance is in the other direction, and one has been directing all of the kindness towards themselves in an unhealthy fashion without considering others, this can lead to a lack of self-esteem, as esteem comes from doing esteemable acts.[3] The practice of noticing whether or not our character traits are in balance can be applied to all of our *middot*, including those of Yitzchak and Yaakov, of strength/boundaries, and mercy.

While it is an awesome practice to look at the qualities that our ancestors Avraham, Yitzchak and Yaakov represented, it is also crucial NOT to compare ourselves to them. The forefathers and foremothers had long journeys and bumpy roads, pains, struggles, difficulties, and family challenges. It is not about aspiring to be like them, as we don't share their journey, but rather to aspire to be like our own truest selves... without pressure, and with trusting the timing and process

## Awesome Blast

of our growth. As the famous teaching goes, the famous Reb Zusha taught his students that he wasn't concerned with getting to Heaven and being asked why he wasn't more like the forefathers, but rather, why he wasn't more like Reb Zusha.

So "self-improvement" can come both from balancing out character traits, and also balancing our striving with personal compassion. But what am I meant to do with that? How am I meant to make that practical, and apply it to my life? Here is a simple angle that really blew my mind! Rabbi Moshe Chaim Eade gave over the idea that self-improvement in the form of *tshuva* is 'when we stop doing the things that make us disrespect ourselves.'

*ALLOW ME TO REPEAT THAT ONE HOMIES: Tshuva means I stop doing the things that make me disrespect myself.*

WHOOOOAAAA. Mind. Blown. In other words, we can strive for improvement as long as the process and result are connected with self-respect. Where it is not self-respecting, it won't actually help us grow. That is a great tip on how to practically apply self-improvement.

I love the way this balance is also reflected by Rabbi Dessler in his book "Strive for Truth." At first he writes, 'our service during the month of Elul must be to throw ourselves into a program of vibrant acts of positive content, to take us from the extreme of moral and spiritual slackness to the other extreme of moral strength and enthusiastic endeavor,'[4] but then just seven pages later he says, but 'we must not despair… the very fact that we are pursuing an intensified action program shows that we have a yearning for inwardness…. and if only we want it, the battle is half won.'[5]

So basically, strive to improve, using self-respect and balance as your barometers, and then know that you already have half a trophy waiting for you on the shelf!

## Notes

1. Vayikra Rabbah 29:6.
2. Zohar, Pinchas 61:368.
3. I learned this idea from my dear friend Shaindel Siskind Deutsch who learned it from her teacher.
4. Page 76.
5. Page 83.

# Breath Work & Spiritual Rapé:

## Elul 7

*Note: pronounced rah-peh, as in the Shamanic tobacco powder that is administered through the nose.*

'To the Kabbalists, it was all about breath. Humankind began when the Creator blew a breath of life into Adam and Eve. What else can only come alive when breath is infused in it? All the required shofar blasts. The sounds of the *tekiah*, *shevarim*, and *truah* can only be made by blowing air through the wind instrument, literally breathing into it.'[1]

And isn't it interesting then, that the root of the very word for breath, "*neshima*," is identical to the word soul, "*neshama*"?

We receive our souls, our life energy, through our breath. And we access connection with our souls in spiritual work through the breath. One is literally the key to the other. If you haven't already heard this idea in your Jewish yoga and breathwork classes, it's pretty mind-blowing.

And following suit, the way we wake up our souls for the New Year is by using that very same breath through the shofar. This reminded me so deeply of the traditional use of Shamanic snuff, called Rapé.[2] Tobacco snuff is a sacred shamanic medicine or tool that has been used

Shofar in Humbolt

by tribes of the Amazon basin for thousands of years and is an essential part of their tribal culture and history. Rapé was introduced to the Western world primarily as a part of Ayahuasca ceremonies, but there are often full ceremonies around the use of Rapé itself.

A typical Rapé ceremony involves a mutual administration by two persons. The Rapé is blown high up into the nostrils with a pipe made from bamboo or bone. This special blowpipe is called a "Tepi" (if another person administers) or a "Kuripe" (self administration). This "blow" can be rather shocking. The intense blow immediately focuses the mind, stops mental chatter and opens the entire freed mindspace for your intentions. Furthermore, this helps with releasing emotional, physical, and spiritual illnesses and eases negativity and confusion, enabling a thorough grounding of the mind. Likewise, shamans use Rapé to re-align with their energy channels and with their higher self, and to intensify their connection with the world and the universe.[3]

*It is almost like the synagogue's Shofar blower plays the role of the Shaman offering Rapé through his/her breath into the nose of the healing receiver. Like Rapé, the Shofar wakes us up, it brings us back into presence, it grounds us, and it is a sacred ancestral tradition.*

## Notes

1. Chabad.org
2. There are different varieties of Shamanic snuff and therefore it can also be called hapé.
3. https://katukina.com/doc/rape

## Birth & Surrender

*Elul*
**8**

One of the classic analogies given to understand the Shofar is that of birth![1] The sounds of the Shofar are compared to the wailing of a woman in labor,[2] passionately crying out from the experience itself and also for the birth of this new baby.[3] So too, we cry out with all of the effort we put in to birth ourselves anew for a New Year ahead. On Rosh Hashanah we are asking to be remembered for life, just as a woman in labor is praying for the life of her baby as well as her own life.

But there is a catch.

One of the most incredible parts of birth is witnessing how the mother ultimately has no choice but to completely surrender if she wishes to have a successful birth. She must surrender—trust the process, trust her body, trust God… and she must do this repeatedly, despite intense pain, overwhelming pressure, and perhaps even fear. It is a true miracle to witness her surrender—as if into another realm, joining God in the sacred act of creation.

Shofar with Mexican Street Art

What does this teach us? The importance of surrender for the birth of anything new in our lives. While it might seem counterintuitive, the act of surrendering can be the key to unlocking new possibilities, especially when we feel stuck or overwhelmed by life's challenges. Surrendering doesn't mean giving up or being passive; rather, it's about letting go of the tight grip we hold on our outcomes. This allows space for new opportunities to emerge without the pressure of forcing things to happen in a specific way.

How can we apply the Shofar birth analogy wisdom to our holiday experience? Some people enjoy learning that the cry of the Shofar is like the cries of labor because they feel it gives them permission to weep, to wail, and to feel their emotional pain during the call of the Shofar in order to birth a new reality for the year ahead. For some, that permission is crucial and if that works for you, go for it. For years I collected piles of soaked tissues next to me as I cried out from the depths of my heart on the high holidays. We even learn from the story of Rabbi Elazar ben Durdaya that one hour of genuine, heartfelt crying out can reclaim our place in *Olam Haba*.[4]

In more recent years I have been trying to incorporate the second part of the birth analogy, surrender, into my high holiday experience. True, we must 'feel to heal,' and also, I couldn't imagine that God would wish that millions of Jews would fall into hysterics and deep pain processing on the first day of the year. Now when I hear the Shofar call, I simply open my palms outward and upward, clear my mind, and just surrender to the sound. I have no agenda, no wish to access the depths of my pain and pleas, I just listen and breathe. Tears may also emerge, but my intention is just to surrender...

## Awesome Blast

# Notes

1. The world, on this day, is similar to a woman sitting on a birthing bed or chair, about to give birth (Sefer Rokeach).
2. Zohar 3:249b.
3. Vayikra Rabbah 20, Midrash Tanchuma, Vayera 23:5, Pirkei DeRabbi Eliezer 32:8, Rosh Hashanah 11a:16-17, Midrash Tanchuma, Tazria 4:1, Tosafot on Rosh Hashanah 33b, Judges 5:28-30.
4. Rabbi Ki Tov, Book of Our Heritage, pg 1047.

# The Portal of Female Anatomy

**Elul 9**

Even more unbelievable in terms of birth analogies is how the shape of the Shofar mimics the shape of the birth canal! A narrow opening[1] which expands and allows for birth. The canal must open up for birth to be possible. As a doula-in-training, I have come to learn the importance of the word and practice of "opening" in birth. It comes as no surprise that the sages say that the time of the Shofar blowing is what opens the Gates of Heaven[2] to receive our prayers and supplications. In birth, the canal and the Gates of Heaven open to bring down this new soul into a physical body.

The vaginal opening is the place from which the beyond emerges. It is the sacred portal between Heaven and Earth. I have it referred to as the '*poch kodesh*,' or the holy opening by a scholar.[3] Similarly, when we ask for miracles and answered prayers with the call of the Shofar, we are asking God to open up a portal from which to bring Heavenly salvations down to Earth.

Moreover, we know anatomically that the mouth, larynx, and vocal chords completely mirror the vaginal opening, uterus, and pelvic floor. This is just another peak into the

Shofar under the cliffs of Tiberius

## Awesome Blast

miraculous physical feminine design that connects the wails of the Shofar and of birth. So yes, the design of the vaginal opening and the Shofar both allow for a portal between Heaven and Earth. *Whoa.*

*But wait, the Shofar-feminine-place-torahs actually just don't stop....* Rav Dov Ber Pinson adds to this idea explaining that the Shofar *is* the midwife of the New Year.

What on earth? The Shofar is the midwife of the New Year? Why? 'The Torah mentions a great woman with a name that shares the root of the word *shofar*—Shifra![4] Shifra and Puah were the main midwives of the Israelites at the time of the birth of Moses in Egypt, and they courageously saved the Jewish people by defying Pharoah's orders to drown the babies. *COME ON, Hashem is almost getting too obvious here! The freakin' midwife who saved the Jewish people, allowing them to live, is basically named SHOFAR?*

Shifra's name means to make beautiful, and that is what she did; she ensured that the babies would emerge healthy and viable, then swaddled and massaged them to foster their strength and beauty. The Shofar *is* the midwife of the New Year, ensuring we all emerge in good health and with great strength. Into its piercing cry, we squeeze all of our heartfelt prayers, all of our tears, our very souls.'

# Notes

1. Psalm 118:5 reflects this metaphor.

2. Rabbi Alan Lew in his book, This is Real and You are Completely Unprepared, expresses, "When the shofar sounds one hundred times (which it does in the traditional service), it blows open the gates of heaven. When the shofar sounds one hundred times, it forms a bridge between heaven and earth, and we enter heaven on that bridge. When the shofar sounds one hundred times, it cracks the shell of our awareness wide open, and suddenly we find ourselves in heaven. When the shofar sounds one hundred times, we hear the voice of heaven in it. We experience Revelation."

3. There are many references to the Divine Feminine, or the Nukva in Kabbalistic literature. *Nukva*—Aramaic for 'female' is also known as *Malchut*, or the lowest *Kabbalistic sfira*. *Malchut* has a female aspect, a vessel, expressing a desire to receive the Light. The *Nukva* is represented by the Letter ה H of the YHVH name. *Binah* is also 'female' and called the Supernal *Nukva*, Mother, represented by the higher ה H of the holy name. *Nukva* and the spiritual connotations that come with it, relate also to the realm of biology. See for example Tanya Chapter 7 about the difference between '*zera levatala*' and prohibited relations between male/female. Also the notion about souls that are produced through marital unions even when they don't result in physical offspring (Elya Rabbah, OC 240:2).

4. Exodus 1:15—21.

# Splitting of the Sea & the Shofar

*Elul*
**10**

So we now know that the call of the Shofar sounds like birth and represents the Great Universal Redemption of the near future. We also know that the future redemption will be based on the first redemption.[1]

The first redemption is traditionally symbolized by the miracle of the splitting of the Sea, when the Jews were redeemed from slavery in Egypt and became a new nation after crossing through the waters. *The Splitting of the Sea literally begins with the waters breaking!* The birth metaphor actually begins earlier in the narrative, when the Jewish people are commanded to put blood on their doorposts. I'll let you conjure the imagery on your own, but essentially there is blood at the opening. *Pretty powerful imagery.* Then the Jewish people go through a narrow channel, and come out the other side reborn. Narrow canal... Shofar? Shofar... Narrow Canal? *You can't make this stuff up folks.* And then, after the holidays, we are born again as a nation on the other side of the New Year...

Shofar in the Narrows

## Notes

1. The prophet Micah said (7:15), "As in the days of your leaving Egypt, I shall show them marvelous things." His words imply that the Exodus is the precedent for the Final Redemption, as the *Midrash* expounds: "Just as in Egypt, I shall redeem you in the future from subjugation to Edom and shall perform miracles for you, as it says, 'As in the days of your leaving Egypt, I shall display miracles'" (*Tanchuma, Toldot* 17).

# Amniotic Fluid, the Womb, & God in Liturgy

**Elul 11**

If the torahs on birth, the portal of female anatomy, and the splitting of the sea *Sho-far* didn't blow you away *(that was a Shofar pun)* how about the fact that the amniotic fluid in the womb is literally called "*Mei SheFeR*," in Hebrew? *Notice anything... Shefer.... Shofar! Whoa... same root again!*

*Mei Shefer* means the waters of *Shefer*. We learned in the last two essays that the root sh-f-r can mean "improvement." In other words, as a fetus, we literally grow in the 'waters of improvement,' or also 'the place from which we call out.' *Perhaps the places where we improve are the very places about which we call out?* Perhaps they are one and the same???

There is more! So now that we are speaking of amniotic fluid, we must speak of the vessel for these waters of improvement—the womb itself. The Hebrew word for the womb is '*rechem*.' So let's learn a bit about this '*rechem*.' *Hold tight—this is about to get even more exciting!*

Both scientifically and Kabbalistically, the womb is the only organ designed in a human for another human.

Shofar in a Cenote

Similarly, the very way that God created the Universe was that first He carved out a space within Himself to make a place in which the Universe could be born and grow.[1]

So here is where it gets even better... 'rechem' is the root of the word 'rachamim,' mercy, and shares a root with the popular name for God, 'HaRachaman,'[2] or The Compassionate One. *It is God's very Compassion that allows us life, growth, and connection, and it is God's very Compassion that we call upon in the High Holiday liturgy! Mamash fascinating...*

Let's review this mind-blow mic-drop step-by-step Womb-Shofar teaching so you can give it over at your holiday table!

⇨ The Shofar awakens self-improvement in us.

⇨ ...SheFeR literally means improvement.

⇨ We see the root SheFer in another concept... the words for Amniotic fluid are Mei SheFeR.

⇨ So Amniotic fluid, or Mei SheFeR, can translate to 'the waters of improvement'.

⇨ This Mei SheFeR is the Godly substance which holds and surrounds us as we grow.

⇨ And as we learned earlier, the Biblical archetype for a midwife is SHiFRu.

⇨ And... this all happens in the rechem, the womb.

⇨ The rechem, which is the root of the Hebrew word rachamim (compassion), is also the quintessential metaphor for compassion, as the womb is a place designed specifically for another. It holds us as we grow, even when we are just parasitic weird undeveloped fetuses with only potential.

### Awesome Blast

⇨ So we can define the quality of compassion using the parable of the womb.

⇨ So isn't it fascinating that in High Holiday liturgy we call out to God as 'the Compassionate One,' or *HaRachaman*?

⇨ And if God originally created the Universe through His own proverbial womb space, then perhaps compassion is also the mechanism through which the Universe is re-created every year? **THIS WOULD THEN MAKE BOUNDLESS SELF-COMPASSION THE MECHANISM MOST HELPFUL FOR OUR OWN GROWTH!**

⇨ So when you hear the Shofar, you can recall the *Mei Shefer* (the amniotic fluid), the *Rechem* (the womb), and *HaRachaman* (the Compassionate One). We can recall the compassion in which we were and are created, in which we grow, and in which we can reconnect to Source and improve!

*AHHH THAT WAS CRAZY. Bam!!! Love myself some yummy Shofar torahs... dannnnng. bH.*

### Notes

1. Kabbalistically speaking, this space was created through the process of *tzimtzum* and the subsequent shining of the *kav* of the *Or Ein Sof* into the abyss. See teachings of the Arizal.
2. Most popularly known in the *Birkat HaMazon*, or Grace After Meals.

# Synesthesia & Tripping Out

**Elul 12**

What does the Shofar have to do with synesthesia and tripping out?

The pinnacle event in Jewish history thus far was receiving the Torah at Mount Sinai just seven weeks after the Jewish people miraculously left Egypt through the Split Sea. It was God's spectacular revelation of Himself & the Divine Infinite Wisdom (the Torah) to approximately 3 million people.[1] It was the world's first philosophical introduction to the idea that the physical and spiritual are in fact one.

According to the simple text, the *Midrashim*, and the Zohar, the miracles that occurred before and during the revelation were nothing short of phenomenal. The mountain had a Jumanji-like explosion of greenery and flowers.[2] Miriam's well overflowed and created wide rivers between the encamped tribes in the middle of the barren desert.[3] There was lightning, thunder, earthquakes, seven concentric rings of fire around the mountain reaching up to the heavens, and thick smoke that went as high as the eye could see.[4]

Shofar in a Mustang

According to the Zohar there was even a mystical purple vapor that spread around

## Awesome Blast

healing people of all of their physical ailments—restoring sight, hearing, the ability to walk again etc. Thousands and thousands of angels descended on their own and in heavenly chariots,[5] approaching the people and offering them crowns made of the light of the *Shechina*, the Divine Feminine.

The stomachs of pregnant women become transparent[6] during the Revelation with their fetuses able to utter the Ten Commandments along with God and Moses. We all dropped dead twice after hearing God's voice, were subsequently reawakened by the dust of the resurrection of the dead, ran miles away in fear, and were regathered by the angels. Some Rabbis even discuss God lifting up the entire mountain out of the ground and holding it upside down above the heads of the nation! The simple text even says that the blue sapphire Throne of God descended and rested on the top of the mountain.

If all of that wasn't astounding enough, there was peace, love, forgiveness, and a unity among the people unlike anything that was ever known to mankind before.

And yet, with all of this, one of the most noted phenomena during this incredible drama was the sounding of a mysterious Shofar. "As the sound of the shofar grew louder and louder, Moshe spoke; and God answered him with a Voice."[7]

"All the people *saw the sounds* and the lightning, the voice of the horn and the mountain smoking; and when the people saw it, they fell back and stood at a distance."[8] *In modern speak, the people must have been TRIPPING OUT YO!*

Many of the Chassidic masters interpret this seeing of sound to mean that there was the experience of synesthesia.[9]

What is synesthesia? According to the *Scientific American*, "Synesthesia is an anomalous blending of the senses in which the stimulation of one modality simultaneously produces sensation in a different modality. Synesthetes hear colors, feel sounds and taste shapes."[10]

So what? What does that have to do with the lessons of the Shofar? The synesthetic experience of seeing the sounds of the Shofar was a hint to the blending, not only of senses, but of everything, all time and space included. When God revealed Himself, there was literally nothing else…. only God (*Ein Od Milvado*). It is like a pie chart. The more Godly awareness, the less ego or seeming appearance of anything else. In fact, even God's Y-K-V-K Name—the one we pronounce as 'Ado-nai'—is a combination of the Hebrew words for 'past, present, and future,' or '*haya, hoveh,* and *yihiyeh.*'

The truth is, there is always only Oneness, but sometimes it takes tripping out to re-realize this. And sometimes, when there is no current psychedelic revelation of God happening upon us, the Shofar call can bring us back.

The role of the Shofar at the Revelation at Mount Sinai was to wake us up from the delusion of duality and help us recall the Oneness. The role of the Shofar in Elul and on the holidays is the same. And the role of the Shofar will be the same when it heralds the full Messianic revelation—a time of universal recognition of God/Ultimate Unity of All.

## Awesome Blast

# Notes

1. Based on the calculation that there were 600,000 men counted between the ages of 20 and 60. So a rough estimate would double that to include women making it 1.2 million. And the Jews in Egypt were known to be having many children. So assuming each family had 2 kids, which is a gross underestimation, you have 2.4 million. Then there are the men and women that were under 20 and over 60, plus all of the Egyptian population called the *Erev Rav*, that joined the Jewish people, so it would actually be a modest estimation to assume there were approximately 3 million people at Mount Sinai for the revelation.
2. Midrash Shemot Rabba 29:9.
3. ברייתא דמס' מדות הי"ט.
4. Exodus 19: 16-25.
5. Bamidbar Rabba 2:2.
6. Midrashically, this phenomenon also happened during the crossing of the Split Sea during the singing of *Az Yashir*.
7. Exodus 19:19.
8. Exodus 20:15.
9. Mekhilta DeRabbi Yishmael, Tractate Bachodesh 9:1, Rashi on Exodus 20:15:2-3, Ibn Ezra on Exodus 20:15:1, Kli Yakar on Exodus 20:15:1.
10. *Scientific American*. 2024. "What Is Synesthesia?," February 20, 2024. https://www.scientificamerican.com/article/what-is-synesthesia.

# Love & Ultimate Unity

**Elul 13**

But wait? Did you ever wonder, how did we merit to meet God at Mount Sinai? The greatest and only claim of open mass-revelation of God in all of history? How did we merit to receive the Infinite Wisdom of the God-Mind? How were we able to receive such a gift?

Rashi, a medieval French Rabbi and the most famous Torah commentator, explains that when we camped out at Mount Sinai, we were "like one man with one heart".[1] The Mechilta[2] also deduced from the use of the singular form of the verb "encamped" (*vayichan*, וַיִּחַן) that all the Israelites agreed and were of one mind. Rebbe Nachman of Breslov explains that we had softened our hearts, we were seeing each other favorably, and finding grace in each others' eyes. He derives this idea of grace, from the word *chen*, which is the root of '*vayichan ha'am.*'

*In other words, it was because of the love and unity that we merited meeting God and receiving Divine Light (the Torah). As my teacher Leah says, if we want to get it together, we gotta get together.*

Shofar in a Forest

### Awesome Blast

*And it is because of our love and unity that we merit to meet God and receive more light today and in the future!*

On the High Holidays we spend ample amounts of time together as a community and we come to see that all of our spiritual work is completely interconnected. We are all in this together. When we remember that, when we look favorably upon each other, that is when we meet God and can soar. *Not only that, but it might just be the way we treat each other, even more than the power of our prayers etc., that reallllly shakes the Heavens.* The Shofar is our reminder to do just that. It is a calling to look around your synagogue and recall our inherent unity, to soften and open our hearts to compassion and love for those around us, and find favor in each others' eyes.

That is why one of my favorite Ram Dass quotes is, "treat everyone you meet like God in drag." I love it, and repeating it helps me put this teaching into practice.

## Notes

1. Rashi on Exodus 19:2.
2. Mechilta is used to denote a compilation of exegesis in Judaism, attributed to or written by any of several authors.

# Jericho—Letting Down Your Walls

*Elul*
## 14

After 40 years of wandering in the desert, the Jews finally enter the Holy Land with their new leader, Joshua. God commands Joshua and the Israelites to go around the walls of Jericho for seven days and then sound seven shofars.[1] By doing this they would be able to:

1. Break down the walls,

2. Expose the enemy,

3. Begin to gain sovereignty of the land.

In this spiritual metaphor, consider yourself as the Jews coming into the land, the walls of Jericho, AND the enemies within. All of it.

Breaking down our walls:

We too have walls that protect our internal enemies, and that prevent us from being truly self-sovereign[2] and embodied. What are our walls? Emotional barricades. Giving the people we love the cold shoulder, not letting our loved ones get close in relationships, not loving fully, not receiving love, not forgiving, not being vulnerable, hiding behind facades, isolating, masking,

Shofar under a waterfall

### Awesome Blast

not communicating honestly, not saying the hard thing, defensiveness, not shining our full soul light.... essentially anything we do to 'protect ourselves,' but that essentially keeps out love, abundance, or success.

Our internal enemies:[3]

What can our internal enemies be? Things we dislike, hate, or disapprove of about ourselves, things about ourselves we refuse to accept, things about ourselves we refuse to love unconditionally, self-harming and self-sabotaging beliefs, behaviors and habits, and our evil inclinations that we identify with.

But why would we put up walls that protect our own internal enemies? Well, most of us have subconscious fears of ego death. *In order to maintain our ego, we hold attachment to our world views and beliefs, and we try to protect the identities/personas that we have worked so hard to create, maintain, and identify with, even when they don't serve our authenticity or growth.*

We can have fears of being seen in certain ways. Fears of loving, fears of being loved, fears of rejection, abandonment, failure, and so on and so forth. And showing up as our true, raw, and vulnerable selves can feel terribly unsafe or even fatal. It can feel scary to meet with and feel the feelings that come with any of these fears.

How do we know if we are protecting our inner enemies? One way to look at this is to ask ourselves, is our persona[4] serving our authenticity, or is our authenticity serving our persona? Our walls are usually found protecting the places where our authenticity is in service of our persona.

## Elul 14

But please, if you are identifying with any of these behaviors, please don't get down on yourself. It is just part of being human—God designed us that way! And we learned to fortify our walls for good reasons; they served as coping mechanisms that helped us survive childhood. They simply may not serve us anymore. And what better time to reassess than the New Year?

But what about the part in the story of Joshua gaining sovereignty of the land? What does that represent in us?

Was all this breaking down walls and Shofar blasts of Joshua and the Jewish homies just a land-grab?

According to Chabad Chassidut, the Children of Israel going into the Land of Israel is a general metaphor for the descent of the soul (the people) into the body (the land).[5]

This descent of soul (spiritual) into body (physical) literally offers us the chance to become embodied and sovereign by owning our traits, choices, and behaviors through our efforts in consciousness. When we do this we infuse the physical with the spiritual, and bring unity to all that is.

Thousands of years later that same shofar call that allowed for the Children of Israel (the soul) to come into the body (the Land), still offers us the opportunity to wake up and let down our walls. We hear the shofar and can ask ourselves, 'Hi my love, maybe these walls aren't serving you? Maybe you can make peace with the internal enemies and love all of yourself?'

## Awesome Blast

# Notes

1. Joshua 6:1—27.

2. Sovereignty can be defined as the intrinsic authority and power of an individual to determine his or her own direction and destiny. Connected to the concepts of radical personal responsibility and ownership of our behavior and choices.

3. According to *Chabad Chassidut*, the seven nations that the Jews were instructed to conquer when they entered the land represented the negative aspects of the seven emotional *sfirot*, or Kabbalistic energy channels that are within each person's emotional make-up. The Jews were instructed by God to conquer the seven nations, representing the negative aspects within our character. The correlation to the seven *sfirot* is also hinted to in the seven days and seven shofar calls. The Canaanites that lived in Jericho were morally reprehensible, and represented that aspect within us that we needed to take emotional accountability for and heal.

4. In short, our persona can be understood as our self-portrayed image, who we wish to be seen as, and who we would never want to be seen as.

5. Likutei Sichot, vol. 9, p. 357.

# The Greatest Ego Death

*Elul*
**15**

I thought to title this book, 'The Call to Life,' since the Shofar is a call to wake up and choose life. But the truth is, the Shofar is equally as much a call to ego death.

So which one is it? Is the Shofar a call to life or a call to death?

Well, let us look at the first appearance of the ram's horn in the Torah: *Akeidat Yitzchak*, the binding of Isaac.[1] Honestly? I feel like barfing every time I read it. And even more so when we *praise* Avraham for being willing to do it. And even *more* when Hashem congratulates him for it. BARFARONI. *What the actual heck Hashem?*

Everything Avraham had worked for his whole life was on the line! Everything he had become and identified with was about to be 'Missy Ellioted'—flipped and reversed in the worst way. Everything he left behind, lived for, prayed for, and preached was about to be flushed down the drain! All of his efforts to go against a corrupt culture—all alone—with the whole world against him and mocking him for years! And he did it all for the sake of the very God who was now asking him to commit this reprehensible murder of his own miracle child??? OY. FRICKEN. VEY.

Shofar in a Canyon

### Awesome Blast

But look at me—screaming to hold on to ego attachments, all in the name of nobility and morality. If I had a megaphone I would turn it on full blast and yell at Hashem at how messed up I think this story is. But that is just the problem. I seem to think I know better than God. I am not surrendering my world view. My foot is down. And I am holding so tight that it brings me to great anger. And we all know what anger truly is… a belief that I am right and God got it wrong.[2] I'M RIGHTTTT GOD!!!! AND YOU'RE WRONG!!!!! The ego inflation is so great that there is almost no room for God at all in my 'corrected' assessment of the story.

And trust me, my upset at God about this story is no different than my upset at God about all of the things in my life that just aren't the way that I want them to be. My reasons are so good I could take God to court.

Can't you see how I serve You God? I made *Aliyah*! I do so many *mitzvot*! I am such a good person! I gave up so many things to live a holy life! (Fill in the blanks with your own protests.) And anyways, You are the One that wants me to be married already/with kids/thriving financially/ released from my bad habits of years already/ truly knowing my purpose (fill in the blanks with your own complaints against God). Oh the righteous indignation. OH THE FURY.

Even though you and I can make a great case for our woes, challenges, and seeming lacks, there is one BIG thing missing. Trust. Trust that God knows what He is doing. And faith that everything He is doing is good and going to be good.[3]

There is room for fighting for our beliefs with Him.[4] But *if there is no room for surrendering our beliefs to Him, it is just narcissism.* He is the One running the show, He is the Only thing that Is, and yet ego tries to squeeze Him out of the picture in the name of what we think is good and right and holy.

What was the *Akeida*? The archetype for total surrender, for enduring total ego death, and for the sake of reconnecting to Life itself.

On Rosh Hashanah we meet our hopes for a wonderful new year, but we also meet all of our seeming lackings, our fears, our ego attachments, and the way *we* think our year should unfold. We are convinced we know what will be best for us. But what do we know? Maybe, just maybe, the Creator of the Universe, the One who holds the stars, is holding our whole lives too? And maybe His path, however it unfolds, is the most perfect expression of his love for us?

Talk about humility and surrender. SHEEEESH.

And what role specifically does the Shofar play in this whole story? *The moment the Shofar enters the scene represents the moment when Avraham realizes that everything will actually be okay, and that God was running the show the whole time.* Maybe we can hold this as an intention for when we hear the Shofar this year?

So was the Shofar a call to life or a call to death? It was a call to ego death, but only because that is the very mechanism that lets us reconnect to Life.

I bless you and me with the bravest ability to let our egos die when they are fighting against God's most glorious plans for our lives.

**Awesome Blast**

# Notes

1. Genesis 22.
2. I learned this idea from my teacher Morah Leah Golomb.
3. Psalms 37:3.
4. As we see in the Biblical precedent with Avraham and his debate with God about Sodom. Genesis 18:16-33.

# Snakes, Ayahuasca, & Kundalini Rising!?!

*Elul*
## 16

*Nili, you have got to be kidding me. What on planet earth does the Shofar have to do with snakes, Ayahuasca and Kundalini Rising?*

I have traveled the world with my three-foot shofar, and there are two main reactions I get. One is from Christians and Jews, 'wow, a Shofar!' And the other is, 'ahhh!,' from the unfortunate freaked-out people passing by who think that the Shofar is a big snake! I had at least 10 'Oh my God I thought you were carrying a snake!' comments on this last trip.

We have already learned that the Shofar represents hope for an Edenic perfected world where the Oneness of God is clear to all,[1] and that the Shofar will be sounded to let us know that this Messianic Era is upon us. But the snake in Biblical literature tends to represent just the opposite! The snake is represented as the deceiver, the liar. It is cunning,[2] it represents the evil inclination,[3] and it seduces Eve into eating from the fruit which gets Adam and Eve kicked out of that very Edenic perfect world! So how could one have anything to do with the other?

Shofar in Tulum

## Awesome Blast

*Wildly enough, both of the Hebrew words for Messiah and snake (nachash) share the same gematria, or, numerical value, 358, which indicates a profound similarity in their essences.* The same essence with opposite exteriors? What?! Well.... trees only grow as high as their roots are deep. The Yin and the Yang are equally measured.

This is where Ayahuasca plays into my thinking. Ayahuasca, a traditional psychoactive plant medicine from the Amazon jungle, is referred to traditionally as *Medicina de Serpiente*, or snake medicine. In the right context (in a healthy, safe, and Kosher environment) this kind of medicine journey can help a person confront their inner face our darkness; shame, fear, and internal 'crunk' that clings to the soul. Oftentimes people have visions of snakes during the journey, or even feel like they become a snake themselves. It can be an incredibly uncomfortable experience, but for those who choose this path, that discomfort and the emotional or physical release that follows can become part of a profound healing process.

This 'serpent medicine' gives us a pause to go deep within, to reflect, and then to integrate what we experienced and learned for self-improvement. So too, the Shofar call gives us a pause to go deep within, to reflect, and then to integrate what we learned for self-improvement. So it is not only the look of the long Shofar being nearly identical to the snake, but also the work of both the Shofar and the snake medicine which allow us to explore similar paths of healing.[4]

This is also where Kundalini plays in. Kundalini is a latent female energy believed to lie coiled like a snake at the base of the spine.[5] When this energy is awakened, it starts to move up the spine, clearing the beliefs, pains, and knots of the past that we often store in the body. The energy can feel unbearably strong or painful, often accompanied by shaking, jerking, or spasms. The challenging effects of Kundalini awakening can be psychological and emotional upheaval, including intensification of unresolved psychological conflict, fear of death or insanity, overwhelming mood swings, heightened sensitivity to others' moods, and confusion. But this can lead to a massive energetic shift in one's entire being—mind, body, and spirit, causing one to move through life in a very different way. According to tradition, an awakening can instigate long-term changes, including feelings of blissfulness and improved self-awareness.

The work and call of the Shofar, Ayahuasca, and Kundalini awakening share a deep commonality as they are are all profound, feminine-associated,[6] spiritual experiences. They allow us to reflect, process, go deep, work through trauma, work with breath & meditation, fall apart, access liberation and potential for ecstasy, experience spiritual bliss, and elevated consciousness.

Wow. The commonalities are fascinating, and so are the polarities that each of these beg us to reach for. They bring us down into the depths, and in doing so allow us access to the heights. *Eize polarities!* The Principle of Polarity is one of the Seven Hermetic principles of the Kybalion[7] and is one of the principles upon which God created the world. So go figure that during the month of Elul and over the high holidays, as we face our dreams for redemption, and pray our highest prayers for life, spiritual growth, and for a perfected world, we must surely confront our darkness, our fears, and our constricted places.

### Awesome Blast

Moreover, according to Rav Hirsch, a religious Jewish German theorist of the 19th century, death came into the world because of Adam and Eve's eating from the Tree of Knowledge by way of the snake's influence. *So isn't it interesting that our pleas for life, our most humble contrition, and our deepest tears, be shed and expressed during the moment of the Shofar call on Rosh Hashanah? The same Shofar that gets mistaken so often for a snake, and ON ROSH HASHANAH nonetheless, THE VERY DAY THE SNAKE MAKES ITS DEBUT?! Yes my friends, you may have missed this massive Biblical fact, but Rosh Hashanah is the very same day we sinned with the snake!!!!!* Mic drop. Think about that one for a while... ha.

And if you want to trip out even more on the connections between Ayahuasca, the snake, the Shofar, and Rosh Hashanah, consider this: I once traveled to Colorado to join a ceremony with a very special Shaman from the Huni Kuin tribe out of the Brazilian jungle near the Rio Branco. I had the privilege of touring with him and a translator who spoke his local language and English. As we traveled through the canyons of the snowy Colorado mountains, I took the chance to ask him everything I could to understand the tradition more deeply. And when I asked him if there was an origin story of how they discovered Ayahuasca, he began sharing with me this story of a man hunting in the forest and he sees all these animals around a tree (reminiscent of Adam in Gan Eden much?). The man was hiding to observe the animals and watched an anteater take three fruits (fruits, seriously?) called Jenipapo. He throws one on top of the lake, one in the middle of the lake, and one on the bottom of the lake, and a beautiful woman emerges (oh look, enter Eve). He falls in love with her. She invites him down to the bottom of the lake[8] and they have two babies *hmm, like Cain and Abel?* which are half people with the spirit of the snake (like Cain after Eve had the remnants of being with the snake…)![9] One day the man then sees her making Ayahuasca, and he asks what it is and he expresses that he wants to drink it with her. She says he won't be able to handle it, but he insists and wants to drink anyhow. She warns him not to freak out, but he drinks the medicine and has a vision of the snake eating him, and of course he freaks out. He leaves the underground world and returns to land. He falls asleep and awakens to find the leaf of the Ayahuasca mix growing by his foot, and the root by his head. He understands that he must mix them together and drink it for further wisdom and insight. If that doesn't remind you of the Garden of Eden, I can inform you that there are researchers in Israel who believe that the Tree of Life was Ayahuasca.[10] And more recently, I have also journeyed (on the medicine) with an Israeli horticulturalist-medicine-man who is currently growing the components of Ayahuasca in the Land of Israel to make a blend sourced completely on this holy ground.

Granted there are a variety of Ayahuasca origin stories that different tribes connect with, but I could barely believe my ears. This Shaman was basically telling me the story of Gan Eden on day 1, Rosh Hashanah.

All these connections are just my theory… but they feel deeply profound and resonate as true for me! And the healing aspects echo in the Torah itself. For example, when Moshe is called upon to accept leadership and face Pharoah[11] (in order to self-actualize) at the Burning Bush,[12] God has him cast down his staff and God turns it into a snake. Then

## Awesome Blast

Moshe must pick up the snake in order to transform it back to a staff, demanding of him tremendous bravery, and also symbolizing ownership of the snake energy itself.

Not only that, but we have a *Midrashic* tradition that the very staff Moshe carried was passed down to him from Adam, from the Garden of Eden,[13] and we know Kabbalisitcally that Moses shared a piece of the reincarnated soul of Adam![14] WHOA. This story is replete with profound archetypal metaphor and could be an entire book in and of itself. But let's jump to another mind-bending comparison in case your mind isn't already shattered into a million pieces on the floor.

In parshat *Chukat*,[15] fiery snakes in the desert attack the Nation of Israel. **WHAT? THAT HAPPENS?** Yeah, but it is a summer *parsha*, so most adults who had a good Jewish education miss this wild story altogether! The nation freaks out, understandably, and pleads for help. The solution? God tells Moshe to erect a large copper[16] snake. Wait, isn't the problem snakes? And now you're telling me the solution is snakes? Yup.

*AND, when the people needed healing from the fiery snake bites, they needed to stare into the eyes of the copper snake pole that Moshe made, and they would be healed.*[17] Many commentators interpret this to mean that in order to heal, you need to look your fears deep in the eyes.

And yes, this story is the source of why pharmacies around the world use snakes curved around a pole as their sign that a place of healing is there!

So essentially, if this is all true, then the medicine of the Shofar, the snake, of Ayahuasca, of Kundalini, of Moses'[18] staff, and of the story in *Parshat Chukat* are all to invite us to go deep within, even to the deepest darkest places of the/our underworld, so we can gain access to the highest sweetest heights of the Upper Worlds. Wow.

## Notes

1. Zechariah 14:9.

2. Genesis 3:1.

3. Talmud Baba Batra 16b.

4. For those that wish to go deeper, one can consider a *chiddush* that my friend Mikey Pauker had. We were learning all night long on Hoshana Rabba, and during the early hours of the morning I shared with him that snake and Messiah have the same numerical value. It blew his mind and then he spontaneously asked me, Nili, now can we do the *Gematria* of Acacia wood? Believe it or not, "*atzei shitim*," the Hebrew phrase that means Acacia wood, totals to 359. That is only one number away from snake & Messiah, and in the tradition, words that are only one number apart can be considered to be of the same essence as well. But why did he ask to do the *Gematria* of Acacia wood? He is also a student of both the Jewish tradition and of healing medicines, and both acacia wood and Ayahuasca—the serpent medicine—contain DMT, or dimethyltryptamine. DMT is a naturally occurring hallucinogenic substance which is also the major psychoactive ingredient in Ayahuasca. So he wondered if the very same wood that was used in the pillars and coals in the Tabernacle were also connected to this idea of going inside to find God. He intuited correctly! Snakes, the Messiah, AND Acacia wood indeed have a connection in numerology and in essence! Go Mikey go!

5. The spine in Judaism is also associated with the snake. Check out Rabbi Efraim Palvanov's class on YouTube called "The Dragon, the Snake & the Messiah" for an in depth explanation of the topic of snakes in Judaism. It is mamash epic and well sourced.

6. Ayahuasca is also called "Grandmother," and carries with her a feminine energy as is traditionally used with the moon, also representing the feminine. And the Shofar is Kabbalistically associated with Bina, another feminine energy from the Tikunei Zohar, *Tikun* 21 p.42a.

## Awesome Blast

7. The Kybalion is a compilation of Hermetic teachings. These same doctrines are based on principles originally explained by Hermes Trismegistus. The Kybalion provides a Master-Key for students to unlock the fundamental and basic teachings of esoteric philosophy. The Kybalion repeatedly references how its seven principles (Mentalism, Correspondence, Vibration, Polarity, Rhythm, Cause and Effect, and Gender) can be seen in the workings of modern science. Although this book was composed in 1908, these statements appear even more accurate today.

8. Kabbalistically we have mention of an underworld that Adam descended to.

9. Check out Rabbi Alon Anava's class on YouTube called, "Were Cain and Abel reptilians or human???—Part 4" to find out about how the sons may have been of a different form of human blended with reptile.

10. Which also follows suit with the Kabbalistic notion that perhaps the Tree of Life and the Tree of Knowledge were intertwined like a vine.

11. Pharoah as representing quintessential evil. Egypt, Kabbalistically said to be the land above which the source of the snake energy lives, and the place which we needed to descend to to be born anew.

12. Exodus-Shemot 4:2.

13. Pirkei de Rabbi Eliezer 40 on the Zohar.

14. Shaar Gilgulim, Arizal.

15. Numbers-*Bamidbar* Chapters 19-21.

16. Copper in Hebrew is also *Nechoshet*, whose root is *Nachash*, or snake. God is so not random. ;)

17. If you, like my editor, are asking, "Woah! How is this not idolatry? Is it because God said to do it?," you are onto the very same questions the Rabbis have been asking for generations… Did God both command the people to die rather than to make idols and also command Moses to make an idol and then for the people to connect with it to heal? I guess you are going to have to just keep learning with me to find out more! It is a very controversial topic, and if you noticed I am glad for your astute nature, but it is not within the scope of this book to address!

18. Also with Aharon and his staff in the courtyard of Pharoah, and also in the story of Yosef thrown by his brothers into the pit as Rashi comments on how the pit was filled with snakes and scorpions.

# The Shofar and the Baal Shem Tov

**Elul 17**

*Note: I have chosen to share about the Baal Shem Tov on Elul 17 in order to help spiritually prepare us for his birthday, which we commemorate on Elul 18, but technically begins tonight after sundown. Also, the Baal Shem Tov was known to be a master of tshuva, and quoted for saying that "most people are a slave to their yesterdays."*

For today's teaching I am excited to bring in the energy of the Baal Shem Tov, one of the greatest Chassidic masters of all time.

There is a beautiful Baal Shem Tov story about the Shofar, and the real intention we are meant to have when blowing/hearing it!

The incredible Reb-Maggid Ari Lesser gives over the story in beautiful poetic rap-rendition... the story is told below in lyrics...

> "One year Rabbi Yisrael Baal Shem Tov went
> And spoke to Rabbi Zev, one of his senior students
> Saying, "You shall blow the Shofar for us all on Rosh Hashanah

Shofar in the Jungle

## Awesome Blast

But first I want you to learn every single *kavanah*
Each Kabbalistic secret of the Shofar you should know
So that you'll have the proper intention when
you blow"
Now Rabbi Zev was quite excited, as anyone might be
He was overcome by joy, but also anxiety
Though elated he'd been designated for something
so great
He was nervous that he'd have to carry this
huge weight
And so quickly he began the task he was assigned
Reading every writing on the shofar he could find.
Soon he knew the Kabbalistic secrets of each sound
How they penetrate the soul, and affect the
world around
So carefully he wrote down notes about every *kavanah*
And then prepared the perfect reference sheet for
Rosh Hashanah.
For in the palace of the King there's many gates
and doors
That lead to many halls and rooms on many
different floors
A palace keeper must have many keys upon his ring
For each one opens up a door in the palace of the king
Rabbi Zev was ready when it came to new year's day
The morning of Rosh Hashanah the first day of Tishrei
He stood up on the bimah in the center of the droves
Of Chasidim in the synagogue of the Baal Shem Tov.

## Elul 17

In the corner of the room his master
looked all-knowing
Standing at his table, with his face like fire glowing
A fearful silence filled the air for they had at last
Reached the climax of the day when they would hear
that shofar blast.
But when Rabbi Zev reached in the pocket of his coat
His heart froze because he could not locate his note
He knew he had it with him when he left his home
at dawn
He remembered bringing it to shul, yet somehow it
was gone
He searched frantically in fear, til it became quite clear
The sheet with all the *kavanot* he wrote
had disappeared
His heart broke over letting down his master who
had asked
And trusted him to be prepared for this most
sacred task.
For in the palace of the King there's many gates
and doors
That lead to many halls and rooms on many
different floors
A palace keeper must have many keys upon his ring
For each one opens up a door in the palace of
the King.
The Rabbi searched his memory, but he could
not recall
A single thing he learned, somehow, he forgot it all

## Awesome Blast

His eyes welled up with tears, his broken heart
just sank
For in distress his mind was drawing up a total blank.
So Rabbi Zev blew the Shofar on that Rosh Hashanah
As though it were a simple horn, without any *kavanah*
In despair, with a broken heart the Rabbi blew
Just the basic shofar sounds he was required to do
Afterwards he couldn't look his master in the eye
He made his way back to his seat where he began
to cry.
But when he finished davening, he looked up from
his place
And hovering above him was his masters smiling face
"Good *Yontiff*, Reb Zev! You blew us all away!
I never heard a Shofar blown as well as you blew
it today!"
Rabbi Zev said, "Rebbe, you must not understand…"
But the Baal Shem Tov just cut him off as soon as
he began.
He said, "In the palace of the King there's many gates
and doors
That lead to many halls and rooms on many
different floors
A palace keeper must have many keys upon his ring
For each one opens up a door in the palace of the King
And yet there is a single key that fits in every lock
And if you have that master key you never have
to knock

With it you can enter even the most inner part

In the palace the master key is a broken heart

And today you had that single key that fits in every lock

And since you had that master key you didn't have to knock

With it you just entered the very most inner part

In the palace, the master key was your broken heart."

Here is a QR code to Ari Lesser's Baal Shem Tov video:

# The Primordial Scream

**Elul 18**

*The Birthday of the Baal Shem Tov!*

*Wait, first, what does primordial mean?* Primordial means, 'existing at or from the beginning of time; primeval.'

The Baal Shem Tov explains that the call of the Shofar on Rosh Hashanah reminds us of the primordial scream, the eternal voiceless call of the soul expressing its desire to return to its Creator.

Rabbi YY Jacobson offers the following story.[1] There was once a king who had an only son. The son was an extraordinary individual with tremendous potential to lead. One day, the king and son came up with an idea together. He should travel to other countries and regions to broaden his horizons and learn different wisdom, to learn what life was like outside the palace, etc. Then he could have an understanding and awareness of who people are and what they are going through.

So his father gave him servants and money so he could tour properly and refine himself through all of these experiences. Can you imagine the tears of bidding farewell to their precious child? As days, weeks, and years passed, the prince's travels led him to substances; addictions and

Shofar at Lake Arrowhead

situations that weren't healthy for him—to the point that the prince sold everything he had to satisfy his cravings.

Now he needed a place to live. He ended up in a far away place, so distant from his father, that no one even knew who he was. When he introduced himself as the prince, they would laugh at him and thought he was nuts. When all the highs were had, and the distractions ran out, the prince was in distress.

He wanted to go home to his father, but it had been so many years. He realized that he had even forgotten his own language! As he came back to his own city, he couldn't even remember how to introduce himself. He was trying to convince people he was the prince, the son of the king that was so honored! But everyone mocked and bullied him. How is it possible that a prince of such a powerful monarch should walk around in such rags and acting in such ways?

Now he wasn't only poor and distraught, but also freshly beat... until he schlepped himself to the courtyard of the palace. But the people in the palace didn't recognize him, didn't understand him, and didn't take him seriously. He was ignored. Until, said the Baal Shem Tov, he finally began to cry out and scream in a loud voice. He knew his father would recognize the sound of his voice.

The king, sitting in the palace, heard the voice and recognized it! 'This is the sound of my boy! My Son! Crying out from his distress!' And all of the pent up love was triggered and aroused, and he ran out to him, embraced him, kissed him, and they were reunited.

This story is a metaphor to understand the meaning of the Shofar on Rosh Hashanah. Because the same story happens Above. The souls of Israel are called 'children of Hashem.'

## Awesome Blast

Even though we have, as if, traveled far away from our roles as princes and princesses of the King, and have become so estranged from our purpose and our pure light, we can never go so far that crying out to our Father with all of our hearts won't stir His love and reconnect us.

As souls, we once basked and bathed in the glory of the Divine Presence. But we come down to Earth—with its tough terrains and distant places—to grow, to refine ourselves, and to develop the skills, wisdom, and character we need to become who we are capable of becoming: an infinitely deeper soul than before we arrived. The descent is for the sake of the ascent.[2]

But we get entangled and stuck. We forget who we are. We get distracted along our journey. The traumas, the losses, the heartbreak, the fears, the insecurities, the money obsessions, the attachments to the physical, the addictions... this journey is not easy for any soul. Our souls get trampled and we trample other people's souls. We get alienated from our true callings. We go so far that the entire presence of our Father is unknown. We forget our soul. We forget our song. We forget our integrity, our authenticity, and our spirituality. And it affects us physically as well. When we are spiritually, morally, and ethically impoverished it is difficult to feel physically full. By dissociating ourselves from our soul and our Creator, we lose ourselves.

But that is also part of the plan. When we reach the point of dissociation, sometimes all that is left to do is cry out from our most authentic, genuine place. That is the call of the Shofar.

## Notes

1. The Baal Shem Tov, Keter Shem Tov, 194.
2. The Alter Rebbe.

# The Silent Scream

**Elul 19**

Rebbe Nachman of Breslov talks about the power of 'the silent scream.'[1] We might have a message or a feeling welling up inside of us, but it is too personal to share loudly or just too awkward to scream in a regular city. Yet, there is so much power in those feelings and in their expression. Listening to the Shofar is our chance to practice a silent scream. In fact, many wise contemporary Jews have commented on the idea that this could be one of the main reasons we are commanded to hear the shofar… to give ourselves the opportunity for this therapeutic spiritual exercise.

This following is from Rebbe Nachman's wisdom:[2]

> Know! It is possible to scream extremely loudly in a small still voice[3] without anyone hearing a thing, for one emits no sound at all. The scream is simply a 'small still voice.'
>
> Anyone can do this. One pictures in his mind the exact sound of a scream, down to its tone. One can enter this till he is literally screaming with this soundless 'small still voice.' Yet no one will hear you.

Shofar at the Lake

This is not a figment of the imagination at all, but a genuine scream. Just as some channels bring the sound from the lungs to your lips, there are narrower channels from the lungs to the brain. One can draw the sound through the channels leading to the brain, till he forms in his mind an actual scream. Picturing the scream in one's mind is a scream in the mind. One can scream loudly with others present and no one will hear a thing.

Sometimes some slight sound may escape. Some of the sound intended for the mind-channels may slip into the vocal-channels, but only slightly.

It is much easier to scream this way without words. If one wants to express words, it is much more difficult to direct the voice to the mind without letting any sound escape. Without words it is much easier.

## Notes

1. Sichot HaRan #16.
2. Sichot HaRan #16.
3. 1 Kings 19:12, Kings 1: 11-13 The following is the context of the passage about the 'still small voice.' "And He said: "Go out and stand in the mountain before the Lord, behold! The Lord passes, and a great and strong wind splitting mountains and shattering boulders before the Lord, but the Lord was not in the wind. And after the wind an earthquake-not in the earthquake was the Lord. After the earthquake fire, not in the fire was the Lord, and after the fire a still small sound. And as Elijah heard, he wrapped his face in his mantle, and he went out and stood at the entrance to the cave, and behold a voice came to him and said: 'What are you doing here, Elijah?'

# The Primal Scream— I Dare You!

**Elul 20**

What is a primal scream? A primal scream is a release of intense basic frustration, anger, and aggression, especially that rediscovered by means of primal therapy. Today's shofar call invites you into the opportunity to let out a primal scream. You might want to find a private spot in your home, or go into nature to give this a try. I bet you met major resistance to this suggestion, I also do! "Where would I even do that?" I hear you. But for those that do do it, you'll get why I suggested it. Profound therapeutic release.

Release baby! Let it go! Let it flow. Go into labor! Give birth! Let out your inner lion/ess,[1] your inner warrior, your inner mourner, your cry, your inner party girl/boy… *whatever is in you, let it out.* Just as there is power in silence, there is also power in volume! There is power in physical vocal release! In expression! ROAR. This might bring up tears, laughter. It is all welcome.

But why? Why do this? Just because the Shofar sounds like a cry?[2] Yes! AND because sometimes we just need to pour out our hearts before the Great Life Navigator. We have the traditional story that Abraham planted an

Shofar with Bison

*Eshel* tree.[3] Many commentators explain that an *Eshel* tree is an acronym for the idea that Abraham implanted within our souls the nature to offer food, drink, and a place to rest to guests. But Rebbe Nachman takes a different angle. He says that the Eshel is an acronym for '*Eshpoch Sichi Lefanecha.*' This means that what Avraham truly implanted within is the ability or direction to pour out our souls before God. It doesn't say express yourself, it says pour forth your soul. Everything that is in there. It is a lot. So, here I invite you to pour out your soul in a primal scream exercise as you hear the sound of the Shofar.

## Notes

1. Talmud Yerushalmi (Taaniyot 2:1).

2. Talmud Rosh Ha-shana 33b, The Tosafot s.v. Shiur teru'a, adds in the name of the Arukh on Shoftim 5:28.

3. Gen 21:33.

# When Words Don't Do It

**Elul 21**

*Adapted from the teachings of Etiel Goldwicht*

We are all familiar with the fact that the Shofar is a calling out and can represent the cry of our soul. That part is old news. But! We can arrive at some new and fascinating thoughts if we break the original idea down to basics. Have you ever thought about why and when a person screams or cries out?

A person cries out when he experiences physical or emotional pain! For example: a cut, a broken leg, a moment of genuine fear or shock, or upon hearing the news (*chas v'shalom*) or the loss of a loved one. We are unfiltered, we don't hold back, we let it all out.

We also call out, cry, and/or scream during moments of sudden joy! Good shock, jubilation… for example at a sports game, when we win the lottery, at the birth of a child, or experiencing awe in nature!

Experiencing enormous sudden joy or pain overwhelms the right side of the brain. Usually we process our emotions in the right side of the brain and then we articulate those feelings with words. When an emotion or experience is big, we are left without words to describe the intense feeling. These are the moments that can't be expressed

Shofar in Palm Desert

in words. These are the moments when the body just lets out a cry, a call, a shout, a scream!

That is the power of the Shofar.

When the Shofar blows, it is a moment not meant to be expressed in words. Or perhaps, words wouldn't even cut it. It is the moment where we tune in and connect to our inner core, to the pain and joy we truly would like to express.

# Wait, We Talk About the Shofar Three Times a Day?

### Elul 22

Do you know that we have been talking about the Shofar three times a day for over 2,000 years? *That's millions and millions of unbroken daily prayers about the Shofar!* Yes, the 10th blessing of the central daily prayer, the *Amidah*, that is prayed three times a day is explicitly about the Shofar! Please note that the Shofar blessing is not in the Shabbat *Amidah*, but it is still included on Shabbat in the daily Psalm 150 verse: 'praise Him with the Shofar.' Isn't it interesting then, that of all of the topics in the world, the great sages wanted us to keep the Shofar not only in our consciousness daily, but three times daily? Or even more if you count that daily Psalm 150. So basically, we're obsessed. *Seriously—tell me this isn't the first time you have thought about the fact that our tradition actually mandates thinking about the Shofar three or four times a day! Fascinating! Now you get why the topic merits a whole book?!*

The 10th blessing of the central daily prayer, the *Amidah*, reads as follows: "Sound the Great Shofar for our freedom, raise a banner to gather our exiles, and bring us together from

Shofar at the Vegas Sign

the four corners of the earth into our land. Blessed are You, Who gathers in the dispersed of His people Israel."

There is another aspect of this Shofar blessing which is pretty epic. My mentor Jack Zeller, of Kulanu,[1] pointed out to me that the Hebrew for 'who gathers in the disperse of His people Israel' is *"mekabetz nidchei Amo Yisrael."* The word *nidchei* is translated as 'dispersed' here, but Zeller has another thought. He explains that *nidchei* can also mean 'unrecognizable.' In other words, those who will be gathered in will not be stereotypically identifiable as Jews. The world might be utterly surprised at who returns Home, and those souls may not even recognize themselves! This is cool in terms of practically thinking about how the future ingathering might look, but I think what's even cooler is the spiritual metaphor for each one of us already claiming to be recognized Jewish souls. We bless the One who gathers the unrecognizable. Are there parts of ourselves that we don't even recognize anymore? What might that mean for those exiled parts of ourselves to be returned home to us?

## Notes

1. Kulanu is an awesome pluralistic organization working with lost and emerging Jewish tribes and communities around the world. Check out www.kulanu.org to learn more.

# How is a Shofar Made & What We Can Learn from the Process?

**Elul 23**

When I first read about how the Shofar is made I was taken aback. First, the horn must be boiled in order to get the insides out. Then it is hollowed in order to be able to hear its call. Can you relate to this metaphorically?

Rebbe Nachman says that when we grow, between each stage of growth we go through a spiritual *mikvah*,[1] but it's like a boiling *mikvah* of fire. It sounds just like the horns' process of getting boiled. Maybe each of those times we were going through a *mikvah* of fire, we too were going through it to become ourselves?

The reason given for boiling the shofar is not only to get the insides out, but also to soften it. Sounds so human. We also get 'boiled' by life to help us soften into our most vulnerable, raw and authentic selves. *I just love the parallels between the creation of a Shofar and the human experience.*

Shofar in Bryce Canyon

And it doesn't end there. What is the purpose of all of this getting the insides out, boiling, and softening it? So that we can hear its call.

Elul 23

So.

Freaking.

Profound.

Perhaps it is through these 'boiling' experiences that *our* call can be heard.

## Notes

1. The word mikvah can be used as a noun, as in, a bath used for ritual immersion to achieve ritual purity. The word mikvah can also be used as a verb, as in, to mikvah. So, one can mikvah, or immerse, in a human-made bath with certain amounts of natural spring water, or one can immerse in a natural body of water like the ocean or a river with a pool. Going in the/to mikvah is also symbolic of rebirth, like returning to and then re-emerging from the womb. The idea is that once we immerse in the waters of the mikvah, we come out a new version of ourselves.

# Shofar Fun Facts

*4 Facts thanks to Sara Levine, writer of JewintheCity.com*

**Elul 24**

### 1. Different Shofars For Different Folks

Did you know that *Ashkenazi* and *Sephardi* Jews use two different kinds of horns, while Yemenite Jews use yet a third kind? According to the *Talmud*, kosher shofars can be made from any Bovidae animal except a cow.[1] While *Ashkenazi* Jews use the simple, shorter horns of the Ram, *Sephardim* only use straight versions of ram horns. Yemenite Jews have a tradition to use the longer, curlier horn of the Kudu, a type of African antelope.

Can you use antlers? No. They don't have the ability to be hollowed out and cannot produce sounds the way that the horns of Bovidae can.[2]

### 2. Hollywood Horns

Watch Return of the Jedi and you'll see some loveable Ewoks blowing shofars as a call to battle. Better yet, it is commonly thought that the sound editor used the same shofar track as was used in Cecil B DeMille's The Ten Commandments, as recorded by composer Elmer Bernstein, who was Jewish. According to an NPR interview with him, Bernstein had "20 to 30 rabbis" on the film scoring stage with

Shofar in Downtown Vegas

him to record the sounds. Shofars have also played a role in Planet of the Apes, among other films and television series.

### 3. Long and Loud

Every Rosh Hashanah, we try to concentrate as the *Baal Tokea* blasts out a *tekiah gedolah*—the longest sustained shofar blast. Have you ever wondered what the longest amount of time that someone has blown a *tekiah gedolah* before? While the Guinness Book of World Records contends that it is 1 minute and 22 seconds, there are videos that seem to challenge it with 20 additional seconds. (For context, my longest *tekiah gedola* does not exceed more than 30 seconds!) The Guinness Book also records the world's largest group of shofars being blown at once—1,022 at the same time.

### 4. Yes, Deaf People Can Do This Mitzvah!

"Look inside a Rosh Hashanah *machzor* and read the translation of the blessing over the shofar. The *mitzvah l'shmoa*, to hear it, rather than to blow it. According to the *Mishna* in Rosh Hashanah, a person doesn't fulfill the *mitzvah* unless they can hear it, but what about a deaf person? Can he fulfill the *mitzvah* to hear it? While most *halachic* authorities say that deaf people are exempt,[3] there are some opinions that state that if a person can hear at all without a hearing aid, they should take the hearing aid out to hear what they can. The *Aruch HaShulchan* says that such a person should blow the shofar[4] for themselves in order to fulfill the *mitzvah*." Good question, no? Have you ever pondered what a person without hearing might do in the case of Shofar?

I learned that God gives us all of the capabilities we need to serve Him. In other words, if one can see, one must use my vision to serve God. If one has a fashion sense, one must use that fashion sense to serve Him. If one has a beautiful voice, athletic abilities, leadership skills, etc.—*you see where I'm going with this.* In other words, if one cannot see, he or she does not need that sense in his or her service of God.

There is a story of a great Rabbi who was the head of his *Yeshiva*, who was learning with his students. Traditionally, when someone known to be more spiritually advanced than you walks into a room, you stand up for a moment to acknowledge them. So students will stand up for a moment when their teacher walks in, audiences stand when a great lecturer enters, and so forth. But when a Rabbi is the head of his *Yeshiva*, he is considered to be the most spiritually accomplished, and therefore would not have to stand to honor anyone, unless another great leader came to visit.

One day, a severely disabled visitor entered the room, and this Rabbi immediately stood in respect. But his students were confused. Surely this disabled man was not even capable of reaching the spiritual level of the great Rabbi. So he explained the above idea to his students. 'God gives us what we need to serve Him. I was given a brilliant mind, physical wellness, and charisma, and therefore I must use all of these abilities in my service of God. Apparently the only way for me to serve God is by employing all of these different talents and resources. This man who just entered was given so few abilities with which to serve God, look how little he needs! He must be on a very high spiritual level!'

This is such a profound teaching because we often look down, consciously or not, on those with different abilities, senses, or resources. But the truth is, they don't *need* those things to serve God. In fact, this realization can awaken deep humility within us. All the talents, strengths, and abundance we've been given? We need them precisely because they're part of how we are meant to serve God.

## Notes

1. Talmud Rosh Hashanah 26a; Shulchan Aruch, Orach Chaim 586:1. See also Shulchan Aruch ha-Rav 586:1.
2. Talmud Rosh Hashanah 26a.
3. *Shulhan Arukh* Orah Hayyim 589:1, citing the Mishnah *Rosh Hashanah* 3:8.
4. Rabbeinu Tam.

# Creation, Co-Creation & The 'Law of Attraction'

**Elul 25**

*Today is the day the world was actually created!* [1]

Rosh Hashanah is not only the New Year, but the anniversary of all of Creation.[2] Not only that, but every day since, and even in this very moment, God is renewing the creative energy that sustains our world.[3] Continual re-creation. Everything is actually new. All the time. Rabbi Shimon Bar Yochai, the Mac Daddy of Kabbalah, explained that literally every single moment is created of new beginnings. That is why the Torah itself starts with the word *"breishit,"* or as Reb Shlomo Carlebach translates it, "with beginnings," to hint to this perpetual re-creation. *Trippy!*

But here is the thing. We co-create not only through our actions, but also through our vibrations. Some might say, exclusively through our vibrations. Maybe you've heard, "your vibe attracts your tribe"? Well, your vibe also attracts all the circumstances of your environment. Your vibe determines what will resonate with you.

Shofar in the Redwoods

*Isn't it interesting then that the New Year, our new opportunity to co-create, is announced*

## Elul 25

*with the sound vibration of the Shofar? I wonder what vibrations the Shofar call resonates with?!*

Ok so if the Shofar reminds us of the anniversary of creation, let's pause and contemplate the following: What does it actually mean that Rosh Hashanah is the anniversary of creation? *Some sages say that Rosh Hashanah is literally the anniversary of the week of the BIG BANG!*[4]

Rosh Hashanah celebrates the 6th day of creation,[5] when man was created. But 5 days before on the 25th of Elul is actually day 1.

Now it gets even crazier. I learned a precious teaching that the Big Bang exploded out of one point.[6] Wouldn't it be interesting to think about which point in the Universe it actually exploded from?

Well! There is a teaching that the whole Universe exploded out of what would be the future spot of the *Kodesh Kedoshim*, the Holy of Holies, otherwise known as the innermost sanctum of the Tabernacle and the Holy Temple in Jerusalem. What could this mean? That every atom of the Universe, and every atom of your body is initially made out of the Holy of Holies.

What if the Shofar vibration was calling out to you screaming, YOU'RE COMPLETELY HOLY!!! How would you or how do you react to hearing that? Does it make you happy? Trigger you? Piss you off? Do you resist it or eat it up!?

Every part of you is holy. And so is everything you have co-created and everything you will co-create. You can't help it. You are literally made, exploded, out of holiness.

And in fact, the tradition itself hints to this teaching. I learned from Reb David Sacks that the great Chassidic

### Awesome Blast

Master, the Jicover Rebbe, points out that the *Gematria* of "Rosh Hashanah" is 861, the very same Gematria as "*Beit Hamikdash*," the Temple. Literally new beginnings, new mindsets, new creations, renewal, starting over, and their outflow are synonymous with holiness. Basically this is one big holy journey.

## Notes

1. Midrash Rabbah (Vayikra 29:1).
2. There are also plenty of different opinions on if the world was created in thought or actuality in Tishrei vs. Nissan.
3. Most explicitly according to the Shacharit prayers (ברכות ק"ש - המחדש בטובו בכל יום תמיד מעשה בראשית), R' Dessler (מכתב מאליהו חלק א), and the Zohar (חלק ב' קמט), but also according to Ramban (שמות יג:טז, דרשת תורת ה' תמימה), Bavli Chagigah 12b, and Tanya (Shaar Hayichud Vehaemunah).
4. Following the idea that the Big Bang can be correlated with God's utterance of "Vayehi Or" in Genesis 1:3.
5. *Igrot Kodesh*, vol. 2, p. 172.
6. Gemara Yoma 54b in connection to the Even Shtiyah.

   וּשְׁתִיָּה הָיְתָה נִקְרֵאת. תָּנָא: שֶׁמִּמֶּנָּה הוּשְׁתַּת הָעוֹלָם. תְּנַן כְּמַאן דְּאָמַר מִצִּיּוֹן נִבְרָא הָעוֹלָם, דְּתַנְיָא, רַבִּי אֱלִיעֶזֶר אוֹמֵר: עוֹלָם מֵאֶמְצָעִיתוֹ נִבְרָא, שֶׁנֶּאֱמַר: "בְּצֶקֶת עָפָר לַמּוּצָק וּרְגָבִים יְדֻבָּקוּ"

# A Hammer for My Hardened Heart aka Holy Soul Surgery

**Elul 26**

One of my personal favorite aspects of listening to the Shofar is just being open to whatever comes to mind, heart or body during the listening experience. As you can tell, I spend a lot of time and energy learning about the different intentions and meanings behind the Shofar. But when push comes to shove and I prepare myself to receive the sounds of the Shofar, part of my experience is just being present to whatever does or doesn't show up. *I often just close my eyes, physically open up my chest area to open heart space, lift or lower my chin, and turn my palms up.*

Sometimes I will hear messages from inside. Sometimes it will make me cry. Sometimes I will be filled with feelings of joy, of hope, of remorse, and sometimes I feel nothing. Sometimes I am distracted by thoughts of work. Sometimes I am distracted because I'm too busy critiquing the Shofar blower's best impression of a dying cat. Sometimes I am distracted by the smells or noises of the people around me. *Just keepin' it real.*

Shofar with the Bioluminescent Ocean

## Awesome Blast

And often, my soul brings me back to a recurring image. I love this image, and so I will share it with you in case your subconscious decides it will be helpful to bring it back to you in the moment of the Shofar call at synagogue.

So I developed a meditation for myself and my students using the following image:

We envision the inside of our chests. But instead of seeing a soft, thriving healthy heart, we see how the heart has been hardened. By life, by trauma, by teasing, by hurt, by pain, by anger, by having to self-protect emotionally. I often see a black, hard, rock-like craggly thing without my life force or movement in my chest. When I hear the Shofar call, I imagine a loving and little hammer, softly cracking away at the first layer. From there I see the pieces of grey and black starting to fall away. This process repeats through the shofar calls until what is revealed is a pink, soft, gentle, unbruised, renewed, refound pumping, thriving, living life-force-pumper. The whole experience feels like surrendering all of my hardness to a holy soul surgery, and I am left refreshed and renewed, with courage to love myself and others again. The hammer gets put down, and I am there to love and fill with blessings that precious, precious heart. The one so full of love and life.

This image came to me independent of a most stunning Torah I heard in the name of Rabbanit Yemima Mizrachi. She said that the only real sin you can have on Rosh Hashanah is not using all of the love in your heart. This struck me deeply. I know loving myself and others more is the core and key. And so I believe that the above imagery can be super helpful for first softening my heart so I can more easily access and feel and give out all of the love light that is in there waiting for me.

I was also astounded to recently learn two other synchronicities. One from Rebbitzin Orit Esther Riter on the Baal Shem Tov who speaks of this idea of *"bitoosh,"* which is the idea of taking a hammer and cracking open as a part of the process of surrender, or *hachna'ah*.[1] Another from reading the Book of Ezekiel,[2] where the prophet expresses that God will take our hearts of stone and replace them with hearts of flesh. *Baruch shekivanti.*

## Notes

1. Keter Shem Tov #96.
2. Ezekiel 36: 26-27.

# Heartstrings

**Elul 27**

The Arizal says that the Shofar transforms judgments into mercy.[1]

All I can think is

"HOOWWWWWW????"

*WHAT?? How on planet earth does the sound of a horn transform judgments into mercy?* Does the sound of the Shofar pull on Hashem's proverbial heart strings? Or maybe one shouldn't ask 'how on Earth' does the sound of a horn transform judgments into mercy, but rather 'how in Heaven' does the sound of a horn transform judgments into mercy? What does the sound of the horn convey? Or what does the sounding of the horn 'for Hashem' convey?

Perhaps it is just the calling out to Hashem itself that evokes the mercy.

For example: if you are in a fight with a partner that you love deeply, the pain of the fight can run deep. It is easy to shut down and turn away. But if in a standstill our partner lovingly calls out to us by our name, it pulls on our heartstrings enough to potentially reconnect.

Shofar in California

Maybe that's what 'hearing' our Shofar blasts 'feels' like to Hashem… that we're still calling out. And maybe it's that very act of calling out that transforms Divine judgement into mercy. Transforming judgment to mercy truly is the energy of the month of Elul, as it is represented by its acronym, *Ani LeDodi VDodi Li*, or, I am for my Beloved and my Beloved is for me. It seems that it is the love rekindled that invites mercy, and that love-call is delivered through the calls of our Shofar to God. Through this turning of judgments into mercy, we merit a good year.

## Notes

1. Rabbi Alon Anava from the Pesikta DeRav Kahana 23:3.

# Why the Shofar is also the first and also the 'Last'

*Elul*
**28**

The first Torah we learned together for the first video on Rosh Chodesh Elul was the Torah of the first shofar. Now in our final Elul essay we will learn about how the Shofar has an element not only of being the first, but also the last.

Why the last? Because tradition tells us that it will be a great Shofar call that announces the Great Day.

Fascinatingly enough, we said that the first Shofar was the body of Adam. Well, the Hebrew word *adam* (אדם) in and of itself is an acronym.[1] The letter *aleph* represents Adam, the letter *dalet* represents David (as in King David), and the letter *mem* represents *Mashiach*. All of human history is represented in the name Adam; from the first man, to the harbinger of the end of times as we know them and the beginning of a new era.

So what happens in this new era, on this Great Day? In addition to world peace, there will also be inner peace within each of us, our relationships, and our families. There will be no more war, nor hunger, nor thirst, physically or spiritually. The whole world will know that God is One, and great love will permeate our existence.

Shofar atop the Plaza Hotel

Elul 28

The Temple in Jerusalem will be rebuilt, and there will be (as we studied in the teaching from Elul 22) an ingathering of the exiles.

One of the key elements of the era of the Great Day, as described by Rambam's famous '13 Principles of Faith,' is that there will also be *tchiyat hameitim*, or resurrection of the dead.[2] *Whoa. That's a big thing!* You will get to reunite with all of your ancestors and loved ones, *for real, in the flesh.*

So what does that have to do with the Shofar? Maurice Kamins, Shofar maker, said, "Shofars are not meant to be lifeless; they are meant to instill life, to be blown. Majestically."[3] When I read this, I tripped out because it sounds like a literal representation of *tchiyat hameitim*. There is a lifeless body, life is returned to it, and through its being brought to life, it has a great emotional effect on all who experience it. This was super profound for me.

There is a Shofar up on a shelf in the Four Sephardic Synagogues of the Old City of Jerusalem that is said to be the Shofar awaiting the Mashiach! You can even go see it! *(I would like to argue that I have the Shofar for messianic times, but ok...)* The *Midrash*[4] explains that one of the horns of the ram used in the Sacrifice of Isaac has been preserved throughout time, and will be the Shofar used to announce the Messiah. So is it the one in Old City? *I guess we will have to wait and see!*

**Awesome Blast**

## Notes

1. Baal Shem Tov Nitzavim 8:1.
2. Isaiah 18:3.
3. jweekly.com/2008/09/18/having-a-blast-s-f-man-masters-the-art-of-making-shofars/
4. Pirkei D'R. Elezer 31 on Isaiah 27:13.

# Crowning the King & Circle Consciousness

## Elul 29

*SHHHH... NO SHOFAR TODAY! DON'T LISTEN if you want to be in line with the tradition! But... if you are watching on another day here is another fun QR code... this happens to be a special greeting from our brothers & sisters of the world... Cuz the truth is we allll want to crown Hashem King!*

It's Erev Rosh Hashanah, and on this day on we skip hearing the Shofar in order to make it special for Rosh Hashanah itself. So what should we focus on instead?

Believe it or not, our main job on Rosh Hashanah is not to apologize, nor ask forgiveness, but rather to "crown the King."[1] Well sheesh... that sounds very vague. And after years of searching, exploring, reading, and learning, I still don't have a great hold on what it means to crown Hashem as King.

Sometimes the day in synagogue gets long. You wish to hold *kavanah*, or spiritual intention, while in prayer services, but it isn't easy to stay in focus. So let's get those visuals going. What do I mean? Envision and imagine. This is my number one personal trick for immersion in profound prayer. Also, recent studies have shown that

Shofar with the Nuns

## Awesome Blast

the mind does not know the difference between reality and imagined reality... so the more we tune into beautiful visions, the more we create possibilities for the magical to become real.

One can envision the prayers of your entire congregation lifting up, floating through the ceiling, into the skies, and up to the Heavens. You could imagine them as Hebrew words, letters, musical notes, or colorful wisps. One could imagine the calls of the Shofar swirling or dancing, being escorted by angels and symphonies, making their way up into glorious places radiating with light. Or one could envision how the people around you might look if you truly saw them with love.

Try to imagine yourself as your highest self. What would you be wearing? How would you walk? Would you have a glow? You could envision your whole community walking hand-in-hand to the Third Temple. You could imagine all of Israel gathered together in unified joyful dances of gratitude to God. The list goes on! The possibilities are endless. And these visuals can help increase the emotional impact the prayers can have on you.

Here's one powerful vision I once received during the Shofar service:

I was trying to open my heart, imagining all sorts of beautiful visions to help me feel more into the prayer services. It was time for the Shofar service, and I was consciously open to receiving any visuals that might fill my mind's eye.

All of the sudden, a vision of alllllll of Israel standing in one huge circle came into my brain. Now we're talking millions of people, so all of us were tiny, but we were all standing shoulder-to-shoulder in one enormous circle. And we were

Elul 29

all holding onto something in front of us with both hands. I realized that all of us were holding and supporting part of a massive crown. It took every last member of Am Yisrael's hands to pick up this crown collectively because it was so expansive. Though I didn't see the actual crowning, I did see us all lifting up the crown together, as if to put it on God's proverbial head. It was a pretty incredible visual. The circle, the unity, the importance of every person needing to be there so we could do it all together. I was truly wowed. The vision stayed with me for a while.

One day, a while later, I went to go pick up some books from a friend, Zivi Ritchie. He was at his mother Lilian's house. I knew that she was a renowned spiritual-artist, but I had never seen her work. They invited me in to wait as he fetched the books, and while I waited I took a little tour to appreciate her painting. I found myself planted before one of her paintings and my jaw dropped.

I was looking at my own Rosh Hashanah vision! There it was, painted before my eyes: A supernal crown in the Heavens with endless little people all around the rim. I couldn't believe my eyes. I didn't know what her particular vision meant to her, but it didn't matter. I just felt like if two of us saw it there must be something true there.

*Perhaps that WE are the crown of God when we stand together?* My own vision had signified that we have a job to do, to make Hashem King, and that that is our purpose here on Earth. In my vision, the circle indicated that we were all in it together, and each person was completely necessary.

It comes to no surprise then that the Messianic Era is often defined as a time of 'circle consciousness.'[2] And that that

### Awesome Blast

circle consciousness is heralded in through the call of the Shofar. Why? The places from where the life force enters and emerges (the mouthpiece and the 'crown' on the shofar) are both circular in nature. Being in a circle means we are all in it together, we are all equal, we are all needed, we are all a part of the team.

*Wait, Nili, it's about to be Rosh Hashana and I love that practical prayer suggestion... Do you have another practical suggestion to enhance our Rosh Hashanah experience?*

Ok, ok, don't twist my arm, Yes I do! I must share my own fun *chiddush* with you, a tradition that I have begun as we circle around my own Rosh Hashanah table. As we said, Rosh Hashanah is both the New Year and also the first day of the new month of Tishrei.

Tishrei is spelled with the Hebrew letters *Taf, Shin, Resh,* and *Yud*. In numerology that would be 400, 300, 200, 100. But there is a special kind of numerology called '*gematria katan*' in which you reduce all numbers to their most basic number. So that would reduce the letters of Tishrei to 4, 3, 2, 1! In other words, we really can do an enthusiastic countdown at our festive meals to symbolize the entrance of the New Year!

## Notes

1. *Igrot Kodesh*, vol. 22, p. 510, Peninei Halacha, Days of Awe 3:6:1-3.
2. Sara Yehudit Schneider, Kabbalistic Writings on the Nature of Masculine & Feminine.

# Prologue to Rosh Hashanah, the 10 Days of Tshuva, & Yom Kippur Teachings

Before we began the essays for the 29 days of Elul we learned about the main characters of the story of the Elul journey—God, and you! Now we will set the stage for the main narrative of what is really happening, spiritually speaking, during the Ten Days of Tshuva. These auspicious days provide precious opportunities to impact one's coming year for all who wish to seize them.[1] To understand the depths of what is available to us during these days, I refer to two brilliant examples from the mind of Reb David Sacks, Spiritual Leader of the Happy Minyan in Los Angeles.

Shofar at the Apple Store

## Notes

1. Isaiah 55:6, Mishneh Torah Laws of Tshuva 2:6, 3:4, Maharasha to Yevamot 49b.

# The Days of Wet Cement

Reb David suggests that the Ten Days of Tshuva are like wet cement. *Remember when you were a kid and there was a sidewalk with a patch of wet cement?* All you had to do was grab a stick, draw a heart, write your name, or press your dog's paw in it, and voila! It is there forever! But once the cement dries? Sure, you could take a camping knife, etch at it for a few hours, and perhaps make a scratch... but it would require wildly more effort.

With this in mind, he suggests that we think of the period between Rosh Hashanah and Yom Kippur the "days of wet cement." The new year and the new Universe are still in the process of being formed, they are like wet cement! As such, the impact of any good things we do is infinitely more meaningful. Hashem comes closest to us during these days, sort of like support staff. He really wants us all to have the best year possible. Now that you know this, what impressions, ideas, hopes, dreams, and prayers would you like to see cemented during this most auspicious time for the year ahead?

Shofar on a Ferris Wheel

Our heart-felt prayers can be the most powerful drawing tools. But it is not enough just to know this; we absolutely must set aside time to pray these prayers in order to make it happen. Especially if it is hard for you to pray your most fervent prayers in shul. If you don't, the time passes by, and the cement dries. My personal suggestion? Block out half a day, or at least a few hours, during these days before Yom Kippur. Take yourself into nature, turn off your phone, and pour your heart out to God.

And just a loving note from the therapist that authored this very self-growth manual... if you notice you are feeling more pressure than inspiration, just put the whole thing down and let growth happen organically. Your personal growth will happen by just enjoying the moment or taking care of what is already on your plate and keeping regulated without taking anything on. You can't win a civil war against yourself. You come before your 'growth,' and guess what? You're going to grow no matter what! *Phew. What a relief!*

# The Skyscraper Metaphor

Reb David brings another incredible example to illustrate a similar point. I call it the "Skyscraper Metaphor." Imagine that you are an architect, and you have been hired to create an extraordinary skyscraper. So you take your pencil and special architect paper and make a blueprint for the building.

Now imagine, after assessing the layout, you decide that you'd rather have all of the windows on the north side of the building instead of the south side. How do you fix that? Simple! All you have to do is take an eraser and redraw the design according to your new plan. Easy peasy.

But what happens once that skyscraper has already been built? Yes, you can hire an interior designer, a contractor, a demolition crew, a crane, a construction crew, switch around those windows and walls… but again, much like with the dried cement, it will take wayyy more effort and cost than if you had taken that little eraser to the page while the building was still in design.

Shofar in Ramle at the Pool of Arches

Now is the moment. We all have a proverbial pencil in hand, and we are free to design our lives in all realms: spiritually, physically, relationship-wise, and emotionally in order to be our best selves and servants of God. May we be blessed to give it our all, to erase and fix that which can be improved, and to design beautiful designs for our year ahead.

# The Energies of the Month of Tishrei[1]

**Sense:** Touch/Sexuality. The month itself and the sense of the month take us all the way back to the beginning, to the Garden of Eden. My teacher Leah says, it's not just what and how we touch, but what do we let touch us? There is so much to unpack here... our relationship with sexuality, intimacy, nakedness, shame, connection with others, desire, and more. Is there a particular aspect of touch or sexuality that you would like to open up to explore for the New Year?

**Tribe:** Efraim. Even though Efraim was the younger of the famous brother duo, Efraim and Menashe,[2] his name is mentioned first when we bless our children on Friday nights. Why? Efraim gave himself permission to excel. While he respected his older brother, he didn't let any excuses stand in his way of shining. Is there an area of your life where you would love to give yourself more permission to shine?

## The Energies of the Month of Tishrei

**Body Part:** The gallbladder is the source of all sexual arousal, as taught in Kabbalah. It is also part of the digestive system. Is there any part of the year that just passed that you would like to digest a little more?

**Letter:** Lamed. Lamed represents learning, teaching, and reaching. Lamed is the only Hebrew letter that goes above the line,[3] giving us the special ability to reach beyond ourselves. Is there a big goal that you would like to work towards this coming year?

**Astrological Sign / Mazal**—Libra, the scales, represent judgment and balance. Libra represents the questions of our fate that hang in the scales over the course of these holy days; who will live, who will die, who will feel chilled out and who anxiety, who will feel loved and who will feel alone, who will be made rich and who poor, who will have *Shalom Bayit* and who will fight... but Reb Shlomo Carlebach teaches that it is really *us* who signs ourselves into each of these books. Which of these categories are you signing up for with your conscious decisions and behaviors?

With regards to balance, the Ramchal[4] teaches that the spiritual root of all illness is an imbalance of the *sfirot*. Perhaps for the healthiest year ahead we can also look at our character traits and our lives and notice which areas could use a little more balance?

**Planet:** *Nogah,* or Venus, is known as the planet of love! This explains the essence of Tishrei, a month of love and forgiveness, a month in which we have an opportunity to get super vulnerable in order to restore and renew our relationships. In fact, we learned that Rabbanit Yemima Mizrachi says that the only real sin you can have on Rosh Hashanah is not using all of the love in your heart. Is there someone you have yet to express all of your love and appreciation to?

**Rosh Chodesh Tishrei in History:** Today in history man was created! We had our encounter with the snake, our first encounter with sexuality, and our first encounter with the very first emotion mentioned in the Bible, shame. *That's mind-blowing for us in the fields of psychotherapy and Shadow Work!* Shame is not only the closet for hiding our worst fears, but also the doorway to discovering our latent talents and greatest light.[5]

Later in history, Joseph was freed from jail in Egypt on Rosh Hashanah. So clearly, there is a lot of potential energy available to us today. You could look at today as a new beginning—an invitation to release yourself from the chains of shame! What might life look like if you decided to just *approve* of yourself with all that you are? Hint: you are the only one who can.

During the month of Tishrei, it is thought that Abraham, Yitzchak, and Yaakov were all

The Energies of the Month of Tishrei

born, and Sara, Rachel, and Chanah were all 'remembered.'[6] In other words, greatness and hope are available to us in Tishrei if we tap in. What strength would you like to discover? What would you like to birth?

## Epic tidbits about the Month of Tishrei according to four super-dope Teachers:

*Morah Leah Golomb ~*

- In the month of Tishrei you have the ability to tap into the source of what Hashem was thinking when He created your soul and the world. What do you think He was thinking? And what's your vision for yourself and for the world?

- "Don't sell God short! You don't know what amazing things He has in store for you!" Can you identify any places where you can dream way bigger?

*Reb' David Sacks~*

- 'What does it mean to return to God? If we understand it to mean that we do things differently, then by definition, I am not that person that had decrees placed upon him. "That" person, well, that is not me anymore.' Whoa, this is deep, have you ever considered what this means?

- 'Rosh Hashanah is a precedent for the whole year, a headquarters... so it's worth really being on our best behavior. Even just for one day.' Are you willing to give it a shot?

- On the custom of eating apples & honey: 'What is honey? It is the fruit of the impossible. Why? Scientists have

## Awesome Blast

determined that honey-bees should not be able to fly based on their body weight and wing size. But the bees managed to find a unique way to fly and produce their fruits. That is why we dip our apple into honey, because what a better way to start the year than by dipping into the fruit of the impossible!' What might you otherwise deem as impossible that you are open to considering possible for you this year?

*Reb Keith Flaks~*

- One of my favorite modern holiday customs comes from Reb Keith. He suggests doing a singathon at your Rosh Hashanah meal. Everyone participates and calls out songs as they remember them. You begin with songs for the New Year, move in order into Yom Kippur, Sukkot, Chanukah, Tu B'Shvat, Purim and so on, including all of the minor holidays and sing songs for every holiday during the year until you end up back at Rosh Hashanah again.

  Why? As you are singing you put good vibes, good intentions and joy into each holiday song, as if infusing all of the coming holidays of the upcoming year with energy and blessing. Not only is it a blast, it is an incredible way to use the headquarters of the year to bless the year. Are you willing to put good *kavanot* into your whole year?

*Reb Chayim of Yerushalayim z'l~*

- "Nothing is random and souls travel together." Look around you at the people in your lives. The people sitting next to you during prayer services, and the people at your holiday meals. Nothing is random and souls travel together. Each person was selected to be in your life and sharing life's journeys with you... perhaps even over the course of many incarnations. This has come to be one of my number one philosophies in life. What if you walked into the New Year in alignment with this quote?

# Notes

1. According to the mystical book the *Sefer Yetzirah*, every month is connected to a sense, one of the 12 Tribes of Israel, a body part, a Hebrew letter, an astrological sign, a planet, a permutation of God's name and more. Here I am providing just a few of the connections to the month to help orient the reader towards what energies are available during the month and worth holding consciousness around for enhanced spiritual awareness.

2. The sons of Yosef.

3. In other words, it is the only letter that reaches above the standard parameter of the form of the rest of the Hebrew letters.

4. In his book Derech Hashem.

5. According to Jung, we repress shame into 'the shadow'. The shadow represents the aspects of ourselves that we have repressed, rejected or denied, often because they do not fit our ideal self-image or the expectations of our social environment. These aspects can include personality traits, emotions, desires, or behaviors that we judge to be negative, shameful, or unacceptable. However, the shadow is not inherently negative. It also contains untapped qualities and resources such as our creativity, spontaneity, or assertiveness. By rejecting our shadow, we cut ourselves off from a significant part of our potential and vital energy. Shadow Work therefore aims to reintegrate these hidden aspects to allow for a more complete and authentic expression of self.

6. Remembered is a Biblical term for becoming pregnant, all after long prayerful waits.

# Can I Bedazzle My Shofar?

*Tishrei*
**1**

*Rosh Chodesh Tishrei & Rosh Hashanah*

There are so many incredible ways to decorate a Shofar! Have you walked through the Judaica stores in Jerusalem and seen the Shofars covered in paint, or enveloped in silver and gold with elaborate designs of Jerusalem?

I have three Shofars: The Shofar I carry nearly everywhere and bring to weddings, my pocket shofar (in case I need to smuggle it into any given country), and of course, my bedazzled shofar that I painstakingly covered in gems one by one while losing much of my fingerprints to superglue. But are there standards? Borders and boundaries to the decor? Or can one have a hay-day and do whatever they please? *Oh my, it just dawned on me that I could and SHOULD make a glow-in-the-dark Shofar!*

So there is a *halacha* about Shofars that are gilded. You might think that in order to do "hidur mitzvah," or beautifying a *mitzvah*, one should cover a Shofar in as much silver and gold as possible! And pretty much you can. With one exception—where the gilding meets the mouthpiece. If a Shofar is gilded, the gold

Shofar at the Carlebach Moshav Synagogue

or silver decor must end before meeting the mouthpiece.[1] Why? That is where we, the human, touch the *mitzvah*. The place of our connection must be simple, pure, and without any ties to anything but the bare essence of the *mitzvah*. Especially without any ties to things pertaining to money.

The blowing of the Shofar is a *mitzvah* that is meant to awaken the heart.[2] And we need to make sure that there is no monkey-business, no confusion, no nothing but service of God. *No amount of money, silver, or gold can influence the power of the mitzvah, and it must be done with purity of intention.*

## Notes

1. Gemara Rosh Ha-shana 27a, 27b, Pininei Halacha from Shulchan Aruch 586:16,18.
2. *Sefer Hachinuch*, Mitzvah 405. See also Maimonides, Laws of *Teshuvah*, 3:4.

# What if There is a Crack in My Shofar?

**Tishrei 2**

Rosh Chodesh Tishrei & Rosh Hashanah Day 2

If a *mitzvah* is done as it is meant to be done according to traditional *halacha*, or Jewish Law, we call it "kosher". So too, the Shofar itself must be deemed "kosher" for blowing on Rosh Hashanah in order for its blower and listeners to properly fulfill the *mitzvah*. A Shofar cannot be made out of just any animal. For example, it cannot be made from a cow. A Shofar also has a minimum length of a "*tefach*" or the *halachic* measurement equivalent of about 8 cm.[1]

Another *halacha* is that the Shofar must not have holes in it[2] or certain types of cracks. There are two types of cracks that are discussed:[3] cracks that go along the height of a particular segment of the Shofar, and cracks that go along the length of the Shofar. So which kind of cracks are ok for a shofar to still be deemed kosher for blowing?

First, I would like to ask you what you think. Which cracks would be permissible and which forbidden? Most people guess wrong!

The answer is fascinating. The rabbis teach that the cracks in a Shofar can represent our sins, and the length of the Shofar can represent the

Shofar on a Sup in the Kinneret

## Tishrei 2

year. So a vertical crack would represent a sin at a given point during the year, and a horizontal crack would represent a sin that carried on for a duration of the year. I bet you guessed it by now.

Vertical cracks in the Shofar can still leave a Shofar kosher because even though we 'cracked' and messed up, we saw the error of our ways, and changed. Vertical cracks allow for the possibility of *tshuva*, for changing our ways over the course of the year. But horizontal cracks render a shofar unkosher because they represent a sin that continues throughout the year. This represents a lack of consciousness, a failure to improve, or less-than-developed desire to do *tshuva*. And these are just not kosher ways for a Jew to approach life. Why? The very nature of being a Jew is believing in our ability to grow and make awesome and brave changes when it serves us to do so.

BUT WAIT. This section cannot end here. What if you realize, much like I do, that the majority of the *middot*, qualities and behaviors that you wish to shift, actually remain challenging year after year? In fact, psychologically speaking, we tend to work on the same things for most of our lives!

The message about which cracks in the Shofar are kosher is a beautiful metaphor. And we can sweeten it a little with one of my most favorite teachings.

The teaching brings us back to the Garden of Eden. The simple reading of the text will have us understanding that Adam and Eve got kicked out of the Garden of Eden because they ate from the tree. The only problem is, as Reb David Sacks says, that if the Garden of Eden was supposed to be so perfect, why did God put a talking snake in it? *Come on,*

## Awesome Blast

*the sin was a total set-up.* So then we have to wonder, is that really why they got kicked out? Because they failed by way of the very test that God set them up for to begin with? Reb Shlomo offers a beautiful explanation, saying that they didn't get kicked out because they ate from the fruit, they got kicked out because they blamed each other. That passing the test would have meant turning to God and just saying, 'I am sorry, I messed up,' and not accusing each other.

Rebbe Nachman says that the original sin is that Adam & Eve didn't believe in themselves. That the reason they were exiled from the Garden of Eden was because they no longer thought they were worthy of being in Gan Eden. He explains that the test was actually: could Adam and Eve mess up and still realize that God loved them and wanted them close? They failed the test because once they messed up they gave up on their self-worth. Think of how many times in our lives we think like this! We mess up, and our self-worth plummets. We give up on relationships, opportunities and self-love, all in the name of human mistake. But we are humans! We were LITERALLY DESIGNED TO MAKE MISTAKES from day one of our existence.

The real test is can we believe that we are still worthy of connection with God and others even when we mess up?

Can we believe that we are still worthy of living in Paradise even when we make mistakes?

My teacher, Morah Leah Golomb, says, 'the biggest secret of *tshuva* is first, you have to not give up on yourself.'

We are the only ones who can decide that we are worthy. We are the only ones who can truly approve of ourselves. And

Tishrei 2

that decision can determine whether life will feel like we are living inside or outside of Paradise.

Swimming in crystal Caribbean waters can feel like swimming in hell if you are busy swimming in self-hate. And alternatively, you could be sitting in a cement box room in bliss if you are sitting in self-approval and trust.

So my friends, even if the crack on your proverbial Shofar goes the long way, you're still a darn ram's horn, and that's pretty bad-a\*\*. We can go get some super-glue and recall how much God is madly in love with each and every one of us, and get back into the Garden.

## Notes

1. Shulchan Aruch 586:9.
2. There is a machloket about holes that spans a wide variety of texts and commentators, for some refer to the Mishna and Gemara *Rosh Ha-shana* 27a-b as understood by Rambam and Ran.
3. Peninei Halacha on the Shulchan Aruch 586:8, 586:9.

# Turn It Upwards

*Tishrei*
**3**

As easy as it may look to make a nice sound from the Shofar, it is really hard for most people to get the hang of it. People ask for advice all the time. *How do I make a sound out of this thing???* I have found there are two things people can do to succeed; turn the wide part of the end upwards, and stop trying so hard. And as it turns out, both of these suggestions will not only yield a better sound, but they are also profound spiritual metaphors for general success in life. I'll explain.

One of the *halachot* about blowing the Shofar is that the wide opening of the Shofar should always face upwards, and not sideways or downwards. Peninei Halacha[1] attributes this idea to Psalms 47:6, "God ascends with a blast (Hebrew, *tru'ah*), the Lord, with the sound of a Shofar."

I can't explain the physics of it, but for some reason turning the wide opening upwards definitely helps with the sound. I CAN explain the spirituality of it with a biblical example. When the Israelites left Egypt, the Amalekites waged a surprise war on them.[2] Moses was instructed by God that as long as he kept his arms and gazed up towards Heaven, that they would incline towards winning the

Shofar at the Grove

battle, but if he lowered his arms and gaze then they would incline to losing.[3] And so it was.

Moses raised his arms and his gaze for as long as he could, and the soldiers were winning. He became fatigued, lowering his arms and gaze, and they began to lose. At this point Moses's brother, Aharon, and cousin, Hur, came to assist him with keeping his arms up. So often we forge forward in life, trying to find solutions in every which way, trying so hard, but we forget one thing...

God is the source of all. Granted God is everywhere, not just above us. But we have a natural human intuition to look up when we pray or call out, and it is no different with the Shofar. If you want to succeed in anything, then the call should be directed upwards. And for whatever reason, this also helps improve the sound. It's pretty incredible.

And now to offer a contradictory thought to everything I just shared in the essay... which doesn't *actually* contradict, but adds a layer of depth. While the truth of the teachings about successful Shofar blowing in an upwards direction is true, there is one element that can be nuanced to be a bit more true in the holistic sense. And I often offer my clients this belief I have that *we can only heal in truth*... So let's get a little closer to the truest truth...

I learned from a medicine woman that the Bwiti Tribe of Gabon, West Africa, often tease Westerners about this very practice that I was suggesting. They say, 'why is that when Westerners are asked about God they look up, or point up???' The Bwiti believe that it is more spiritually accurate to point inwards, into our center, indicating that we find God inside of ourselves, and not outside of ourselves. I loved learning

### Awesome Blast

this! *Have you ever laughed at the notion that we point outside of ourselves to signal where God can be found?*

It is actually kind of funny when you think about it! So maybe point in with one finger and up with the other? For a greater measure of truth we can hold both of the ideas of God above (and below and everywhere) and God within at the same time. As the Kabbalists teach, God fills all worlds and surrounds all worlds.[4]

## Notes

1. A series of books on Jewish Law authored by the contemporary Rabbi, Rav Melamed of Yeshivat Har HaBracha, *shlita*.
2. Exodus 17: 8-13.
3. Exodus 17:11.
4. The *Tanya*, Chapter 41 teaches, *Mimale Kol Alamin, V'Sovev Kol Almin*—"You (God) fill all worlds and You surround all worlds"

# Maybe We Don't Have to Try So Hard?

*Tishrei* **4**

The biggest mistake I see people making when they want to succeed in making a beautiful sound out of the Shofar is to blow with all their might! I have to refrain from giggling sometimes when their heads begin to shake from effort. Because that is not what is needed to make a beautiful sound. In fact, it is just the opposite.

What I have learned over the years of playing the Shofar is that the more gently I can release the air, the more powerful and sustained a sound I can make. I see some serious parallels here with our efforts in life as well.

Do you hear yourself asking, "but I am trying so hard, why aren't things working out the way I want them to?" Just like the person trying so hard to make a good blast out of a Shofar to no avail, sometimes we are busy trying sooooo hard at life that we end up in more tension, stress, and despair. Many of us carry beliefs such that we must exert ourselves until exhaustion in order to succeed. Yet I find in my work as a therapist that the more we handle life situations, emotions, and work with a sense of rest,

Shofar at the Hollywood Sign

## Awesome Blast

surrender, calm and gentleness, the more we can succeed and succeed sustainably.

It is one of life's great paradoxes. *Much like the analogy of the Chinese finger trap; it actually gets more difficult the more one tries.* Another real-life analogy I have found for this is when trying to open a clasp on a piece of jewelry when in a rush or at the end of the night. Sometimes I have to pause and breathe and patiently, gently take my time... and only then am I able to successfully open that which seemed nearly impossible to open, and was totally a frustration. It is a deep lesson in both patience and not forcing.

It is amazing to watch people try to blow the Shofar again after they get the instruction to relax. It works wonders!

# It Doesn't Have to Be Perfect, Just Don't Give Up

## Tishrei 5

For those of us that have been in synagogue on Rosh Hashanah, you know that you sometimes have to put on your game-face, act like an adult, and stifle the giggles because the Shofar sounds can be pretty funny and squeaky. But somehow those funny noises, the flatulent sounds and airy attempts, don't seem to bother God. But most of us relate that it irks us and can distract us from our *kavanah* (spiritual intention) while listening. You might even recall when the person next whispered, "I could play it better than *that!*"

But in truth there are no rules about the perfection of the sounds! Because God isn't into perfection. He is into our hearts.

The Shofar player is not chosen based on which congregant is in the local philharmonic orchestra who can truly perform. The real qualification for who is chosen to play the Shofar for the congregation is someone who is God-fearing.

Shofar at the Santa Monica Pier

"God-fearing" is like Biblical slang for someone who has respect for the type of world that God wishes we will co-create: a world of sincerity, and a world of not-giving-up. Not a world of impressive results. Our work in this world, like the Shofar blasts, does not have to be perfect. In fact, my teacher Chana Rachel Frumin often says, "perfectionism is the enemy of 'good enough." Perfectionism will keep us in judgment and away from completing our tasks and our personal offerings in this world.

Moreover, the Peninei Halacha explains that "the shofar-blowing" is not to be divided among several people. Rather, one person blows all the shofar blasts, as 'one who begins a *mitzvah* should be encouraged to complete it."[1] It doesn't say one has to complete it with booming glorious blasts. It says that one should be encouraged to complete it. That's it. That they should just go for it and not give up.

So what can we learn from this to help us navigate our lives in this year ahead? Or even the day ahead? Or just how to approach life? It is not about how things sound or look that matters in the eyes of God. It is the respect through which we walk through the world that finds favor in His Eyes. And what is important is the willingness not to give up, and to see a mitzvah to its completion. Just keep going. And notice if perfectionism is present, because that might be the very thing that has a person not seeing things through.

## Notes

1. Rema 585:4.

# The Shofar Represents Strength

*Tishrei*
**6**

People of all ages enjoy getting to hold the Shofar, especially kids. The one I carry around is really long and has two twists to it, so not only is it a spectacle to see, but people also want to feel its texture and its weight. It sometimes drops to the floor in the exchange and people look absolutely horrified, 'Oh no! Did it break? Did I break it?'

People seem so confused when I don't look worried about it hitting the ground. It is so sweet that they are concerned, but because I have spent so much time traveling with this Shofar I tend to laugh and explain to them, 'it's allll good, I am pretty sure nothing happened to it... it is an animal horn, this thing is STRONGGG!'

*In fact, Shofars are remarkably strong.*

The sages say that the Shofar represents power and strength. Why did God choose to make the symbol of the New Year a symbol of power and strength? Perhaps to remind us of our own remarkable strength and abilities to start anew? Perhaps to help us recall the power of our prayer if we chose to call

Shofar with the coolest tree in Beverly Hills

**Awesome Blast**

out to Him? Perhaps to remind us that like a Shofar, no matter how many times we crash and fall that our spirit is truly unbreakable?

# Wait, We Do Our Holiest Work Through the Physical?

*Tishrei*
# 7

Did you ever think about the fact that the peak *spiritual* service of the High Holidays is performed using an *animal* horn? Usually, animals in Judaism represent the physical. Wouldn't it make more sense if the peak of our worship was through some outpouring of our soul or some spiritual instrument? But God chose part of an animal instead. Why?

Why is it that our voices, our prayers, and our hopes are raised through the sound of the horn of an animal?

It has to do with the idea that using the physical in service of the spiritual is truly the highest form of *avodah*.

Anyone with self-discipline can go sit alone on a mountain-top undisturbed, meditate, and feel spiritual. That's a great plan. And it is admirable. But it is not the highest. What is higher than a mountain-top meditation? Changing dirty diapers with love, getting stuck in traffic with patience, eating healthfully, working through addiction with empathy, or figuring out how to make it through the

Shofar on Sunset Blvd

### Awesome Blast

challenges of our physical existence while rooting in faith. Those are the highest forms of self-discipline.

We are not meant to just be spiritual, or we already would be. We were given animal bodies, and according to Chabad Chassidut, we were also partially given animal souls,[1] for a reason. We are specifically meant to engage with our physicality and our animalistic nature in holy ways.[2] It then comes to no surprise then that God chose a physical animal instrument, the Shofar, for the great call of Rosh Hashanah which is the practical start of another very practical year of life. And also that God chose the Shofar for heralding the times of the Messianic Era, when the physical and spiritual are united and revealed as One.

## Notes

1. Tanya, Chapters 1, 2.
2. Tanya, Chapter 37.

# Kabbalistic Intentions on Balance, Healing, and Unification: An Advanced Teaching

*Tishrei*
**8**

Ok. Buckle up. Did you know we can alter our consciousness through tuning into Divine energy channels? And that the Zohar[1] explains that on a deeper level, that is what the call of the Shofar is all about?!

These energy channels, the *sfirot*, are mapped out in the Kabbalistic Tree of Life; a diagram that explains the 'spiritual DNA' of the world. While we cannot always alter our physical DNA, we *can* alter our spiritual DNA through altering our consciousness. The Ramchal[2] explains that all illness, or 'dis-ease,' is an imbalance in the energies of the *sfirot*, and therefore all healing comes about through balancing them.

There are three main calls of the Shofar, the *tekia*, the *shvarim*, and the *terua*. The sounds represent three of the primary energies in our personality that require balance for emotional and spiritual health: *chesed*, *gevurah*, and *tiferet*.[3]

Shofar at the Dorothy Chandler Pavilion

The *tekia, the single* blast, is rooted in the *sefira* of *chesed*. Chesed (simply put) is loving-kindness, or the active, loving influencing power of the Divine. The *tekia* reminds the blower/listener that if he or she performs acts of kindness even despite much resistance, they can avert even fierce anger.

The *shevarim*, the three short blasts, are related to the *sefira* of *gevurah*. This is because the word *shevarim* means 'broken,' and it takes strength (*gevurah*) to break something. The *shevarim* reminds the blower/listener to tap into the vulnerable strength required to feel the feelings of their contrite and broken hearts. As the Kotzker Rebbe said, "there is nothing more whole than a broken heart."

The *terua*, or nine short blasts, are connected to the *sfira* of *tiferet*. *Tiferet* can be defined as compassion, or beauty. The *terua* is a reminder to the blower/listener that with enough compassion for self and others we can break the power of the negative spiritual energies of the *Sitra Achra*.

Like the fragmented *terua*, the *Sitra Achra*, or 'the other side,' wishes for us to perceive everyone else as 'on the other side,' thereby diminishing our compassion and fragmenting the unity in the world. By choosing compassion, we stop making enemies out of friends and enemies of ourselves, and instead restore the balance of *tiferet* and beauty in our lives, and in the world.

Who knew that listening to the calls of the shofar were really invitations to balance our emotional attributes of lovingkindness, strength, and compassion, return to personal health, and restore the balance in mankind?!

Bonus Kabbalistic thoughts on Unification:

The word *"shofar"* itself is grammatically feminine and therefore hints at the feminine *sefira* of *bina,* or energetic channel of 'understanding.' *Wait a second Nili, you're telling me the word Shofar is an embodiment of a feminine energy? But the physical Shofar itself seems so... phallic!*

I haven't read this anywhere, but this contrast struck me with a deep thought. We know that all Kabbalistic unification happens due to unifying feminine and masculine energies. So perhaps the fact that the word is feminine and the instrument itself seems masculine could imply that the ritual also accomplishes some sort of unification of Hashem's name. It makes me wonder what potential for new life the very ritual of the Shofar creates the possibility for...

## Notes

1. A central book of Kabbalistic teachings.
2. Derech Hashem.
3. Tikunei Zohar, *Tikun* 21 p.42a.

# Preparing for Kol Nidre: a Battle Call on the Inner Critic

**Tishrei 9**

Historically, the Shofar was a battle call! For example: in the book of the prophet Jeremiah[1] when the enemy army sweeps down upon Judah from the north, God signals a messenger to sound the Shofar to alarm the people of Judah, allowing them to flee to their walled cities for safety as battle came upon them. As the verse describes: the enemy forces prepared to pounce on us like an enraged lion. "What has been will be again, what has been done will be done again; there is nothing new under the sun."[2] At present, there remains a spiritual enemy force that wishes to pounce on us, do battle with us, and destroy us. Who is this main enemy of our generation?[3] The inner critic!

Wait, the Shofar can be a battle call against the inner critic?

How?

And what does this have to do with preparing for *Kol Nidre*, the opening service of Yom Kippur? Huh? I thought *Kol Nidre* was about the annulment of all of the legal vows we have made this year? Yes, technically. But spiritually

Shofar at a Bonfire

speaking, Rabbi Shlomo Carlebach suggests, what vows did we really take this last year that need to be annulled? The vows against ourselves and what we can and can't be and do. We vow we can't do *this*, or we aren't like *that*. We let critical comments come out of our mouths about our appearance, talents, possibilities, and capabilities that break us down even before we have the chance to dream of what can truly become and accomplish!

*Wait a sec, Nili. This sounds really woo-woo. Did that Rabbi just make that up? Is there a source or context for this teaching?*

There is. Not only that, but it truly changed my life and shifted my paradigm of reality. Let's go a step deeper into this teaching…

Rabbi Shlomo Carlebach, the sweet-singer of Israel, the Rabbi of the hippies, the one who taught us that everyone is precious, brings an incredible *vort* from the Chassidic Rebbe, the Ishbitzer, in spiritual preparation for Yom Kippur.

It is based on a Midrashic tale[4] that goes as follows. When God created the world and said the Hebrew words, "*na'aseh adam,*"[5] or "let Us create man," he was inviting everything that had already been created (aka, 'Us') to contribute to this new creation called "man." Every creation was so excited to be a part of the pinnacle of creation! This explains why we have so much of the created world within us, water, the elements, etc.

But some of the angels, on the other hand, expressed great concern! Two angels by the name of Uza and Az'el specifically. 'Man? Who needs man? They will destroy the environment, they will ruin the harmony! No way, God… this is not a good idea.'

## Awesome Blast

Well, what ended up happening is that these angels still ended up contributing of themselves to the creation of man. But what did they contribute? This voice. The inner critic!!! This negative spin. Condescension. This, "Who needs man?" This sad ability to look at ourselves in the mirror and think, *'uch, who needs me?'* Or, at another creation, or another human and think, 'uch, who needs them anyway?'

He explains that this idea actually lays the foundation for all war. For how could we kill another if we thought that they were truly needed and worthy?[6]

In fact, the very names of these angels, Uza and Az'el combine to form the Hebrew word for hell, or '*Azazel.*' *Whoa.*

So if this hellish voice of "who needs them anyway" is within us, how do we return to worthiness and belief in how very needed we truly are?

The answer? Consciousness of the voice of the inner critic. Awareness that the voice is a lie and it is there for the very purpose of finding our way back to worth. God wanted to create us, knowing full-well all the destruction and chaos we would personally and collectively create… and He still did it. Because we are worth it. Because we are needed. Because we are the final partners in healing this whole story. And how do we do it? Yom Kippur lends us two powerful insights to consider in order to protect ourselves in the battle against this voice.

First, we know we are meant to emulate God. And over the course of Yom Kippur, God is consistently referred to as 'The God of Compassion.'[7] We can choose voices of compassion instead of the hellish voices that attempt to seduce us out of self-worth, or into condescension of others. If, for example, I hear the inner critic say something like, "wow Nili you didn't get anything done today," I can ask myself instead, "what would the voice of compassion say?"

The second way to protect ourselves from this voice is by annulling it, as we do in Kol Nidre. I learned from my teacher, Morah Leah Golomb of the Carlebach Moshav, the following: Why do we begin the holiest day of the year with annulling our vows? That is what we are technically doing during the Kol Nidre prayer. *And anyhow, it's 2025, who is making vows? What vows?*

She explains that these vows are really the vows we take against ourselves and others. "I can't do this." "I'm so not creative." "I could never teach." "I am lazy." "They are just that kind of person." "They'll never get it." And so on and so forth. Condescension at its finest… the modern day voices of Uza and Az'el… 'who needs them? who needs me? I am not worth it. They are not worth it.'

On Yom Kippur we remember that nothing could be further from the truth. No matter what we have done, we can be forgiven. The Creator of the Universe asks us to choose life![8] Because He wants us. Because He needs us. Because we are worth it. The Heavenly voice calls out to beckon us back to a Heavenly existence in which we realize just how needed and worthy we truly are.

The battle is on. And I say, "you are fired, inner critic! Goodbye to all of the vows and promises that swore what I could, couldn't, and can't do. You are officially annulled. All those (*kol*) vows (*nidre*) I took? Adios. Ciao. Fare thee well."

Awesome Blast

# Notes

1. Jeremiah Chapter 4.
2. Ecclesiastes 1:9.
3. This is not explicitly a Torah idea, it comes from my personal research and 12 years of working as a Spiritual Psychotherapist, noticing trends. It is my personal belief that the inner critic, or as I like to call it, "the voice of hard on ourselves" is the greatest enemy to our content and happiness.
4. Lev HaShamyim "Uza and Az'el," Rabbi Shlomo Carlebach.
5. Genesis 1:26.
6. Please don't take this as a modern day political commentary, I live in Israel and I am deeply grateful for every member of the IDF protecting us and defending our right to exist. Please take it metaphorically.
7. Psalms 86:15.
8. Deuteronomy 30:19.

# You're Already Forgiven

*Tishrei*
**10**

Yom Kippur is upon us, and we get to hear the FINAL Shofar blast of the holiday season. But the weirdest thing happens after we blow that final Shofar on Yom Kippur. After we have fasted and prayed our hearts out for an entire day of chest-pounding, tears, and tissues, we say "forgive us" one last time.

Huh, but I thought we were already forgiven by this point in the service???

Rabbi Shlomo Carlebach taught that the reason we ask for forgiveness one last time is to repent for the fact that we don't truly believe that we are forgiven. God can and did let go, but have we?

That final Shofar blast at the end of the service is one final wake-up call to realize that God loved us before, during, and after any wrong-doings we did. Sometimes this last Shofar call signifies the highest spiritual aspiration of the whole High Holiday season... just to believe with full heart that we are pure, untainted by our past, and unconditionally loveable.

Shofar at the Orient Hotel

## Awesome Blast

Even if we messed up, even if we created a mess, as long as we have put in our *tshuva* efforts, we are completely forgiven.

Rav Doniel Katz offers a beautiful metaphor to explain this. Imagine you are in a simple room, with a small open window on the wall with a ray of sunshine is shining in. Now imagine taking a huge bucket of black paint and throwing it all over the ray of light. What happens? Nothing. The paint falls to the floor.

What if you take more and more buckets of black paint and go wild, Jackson Pollock style on the room? What happens to the ray of light? Nothing. That is our soul, pure and untainted. Perhaps we have to clean up the mess in the room, but nothing can touch that ray of light.

The clean up is the work we did over the holiday season. That was what we had to do to take care of the messes we have made and clean up our act so we will make less mess in the future. Once we clean, the room is clean and we are forgiven. And our souls? They remain as they ever were—pure, holy, loveable, and forever connected to, and part of, God and His Unconditional Love.

Wake up one last time, *wake up! You were forgiven all-along! Now can you forgive yourself? Completely???*

Abraham Hicks explains that the only reason we ever feel bad about ourselves is because our feelings don't align with how God[1] feels about us and so it is uncomfortable to feel untrue feelings. Falsehood doesn't feel right in a reality of Truth. God is madly in love with us—like a parent to a new born baby. Maybe that kind of love has felt hard to remember, or even believe, until this very moment. But with Yom Kippur upon us, can you contemplate this idea that God is madly in

# Tishrei 10

love with you, was completely madly in love with you, and will be completely and madly in love with you forever and ever? *Wow.*

*If you want to pause in and breathe into these loving vibrations,*

*here is a cantorial piece I sang with a dear friend to usher in Yom Kippur.*

*You can close your eyes, imagine all of the Divine love that is pouring down onto us,*

*and lift it right back up to God with the sweetness of your prayers.*

*Tzom Kal, easy fast, sweet friends.*

*May you be written and sealed in the Book of Good Life.*

*'Ya'aleh....'*

## Notes

1. Abraham Hicks prefers the term Source.

# Conclusion and Preparation for Sukkot

*What "Now"?*

What now? You've read the 40 'Shofar Intentions.' Elul, Rosh Hashanah, and Yom Kippur have come and gone. You know that I put all of these ideas into words with the dream that my readers and friends will develop a greater love and awareness of the epically-cool awesomeness of the Shofar, and all that it represents in our lives both personal and Universal.

*You now know that holding consciousness around the Shofar and its call to the Great Day is holding consciousness of the meaning and purpose of our lives.*

The blessing of living our daily lives, deeply believing that Mashiach can come any moment

and that we have a role in it,

*is* that gift of purpose.

Every day you can wake up knowing you are here for that most precious reason.

Shofar at Ein Gedi

May that lead you to deeply want to infuse your life's actions with meaning. There is no greater blessing. May this consciousness fill

## Conclusion and Preparation for Sukkot

you with an unbreakable hope in God, in yourself, and in those around you. May it reinforce your faith, and empower you with unwavering belief in your own importance.

*Ok, that's cute. But how does one integrate all of this wisdom? And wait a second, the question that prompted this conclusion wasn't "now what," but "what 'NOW'?"*

I was on an Iboga (plant medicine) retreat in Costa Rica with a very sincere mission to heal some of my old painful patterns and shadowy stuff... all of the things that allowed me to hold a secret title of "Queen of Misery," for the first 38 years of my life.

So there I was, the only Jew at the retreat center and so many of the dinner discussions were questions about Judaism. The facilitators were genuinely curious and interested to know more. Of course it did not take long before my enthusiastic passion about the Shofar and Mashiach were spilling out of my mouth. I was telling them that there are even people in New York and Israel that are so excited about hastening the Messianic Era that they have a chant that they sing and dance to through the streets! "We want Mashiach now, we want Mashiach now!" I began to bounce around and sing it for them.

The kind-hearted non-Jewish yogi facilitator, Elizabeth Bast, looked at me with her big doe-eyes, and asked in the sweetest voice, 'Oh, does that mean, like, bringing Mashiach consciousness into every 'now'?

I nearly fell off my chair. I had never thought of it like that before. And she was so so right! Traditionally the chant of "we want Mashiach now" was more of a demand of God,

175

### Awesome Blast

representing how much we want a world of peace as soon as possible. But this woman gave a whole new light to it, and a way more accurate meaning that both aligns with spiritual truth, and is the only way to actually arrive at a Messianic Era.

Us new-age spiritualist folk know deep in our bones that ALL THERE IS IS NOW.[1] We also know that there is a collective consciousness. The collective consciousness is always made of all of the different 'now' consciousnesses of the members of humanity, of you and I. (If this concept is new to you, please re-read it again and again until you get it.)

What she was implying when she asked if the chant was about bringing Mashiach consciousness into 'every now' was, 'is the chant about tuning into the vibes we expect to experience when Mashiach comes in every now/moment?' The answer is yes, and this *is* the answer. To everything.

If we really want to *bring* Mashiach, the most direct path is through *being* in Messianic vibes right now. In kindness, in love, in respect, in awe, in splendor, in peace, etc. This way, if all of us are vibing these vibes, then the collective consciousness would be Messianic. *And there you have it folks... voila, the Messianic Era.*

I was so enamored with this idea that I began experimenting with applying this teaching to playing the Shofar. I wanted to see if being in the moment—completely in the moment—would have any effect on the sound or experience of blowing the Shofar. I used to be very committed to praying for Mashiach when I blew, but I decided to try something new, to just be in the now.

Do you hear the transition? My experience shifted from *THINKING* about Mashiach, to *BEING* in Mashiach vibes, to

## Conclusion and Preparation for Sukkot

just BEING present. *And the strangest phenomenon began to occur...* Any time I play Shofar in the 'now' it is almost as if the wind in my lungs does not run out. I can keep playing and playing and playing, and yes, it does end, but the amount of time I can play for has nearly doubled, and with way less effort. Thought stops, and I am simply present.

So how does one get off this freight-train-of-the-brain?

How does one stop thinking?

Usually when we consciously breathe, thought begins to soften, until it is distant enough to allow us to return to the present moment.

Now I don't mean breathe and think about your to-do-list. I mean really, really breathe and stay focused on your breath like your life depends on it. Because it does—literally, and spiritually.

🗝 The key that unlocks the door to presence is breath.

*What happens next?*

Usually when we become present, we notice our surroundings, our body, its magnificent miraculous functioning, and then we can't help it, we start to feel grateful.

🗝 The key that unlocks the door to gratitude is presence.

Then, when we begin to feel grateful, we can't help it, we start to feel joy.

🗝 The key that unlocks the door to joy is gratitude.

Breath. Presence. Gratitude. Joy.

There you have it.

### Awesome Blast

*So isn't it just oh-so-interesting that the whole Shofar ritual is inextricably linked to, inseparable from, impossible without, breath? No breath, no Shofar call. Yes breath, the call of life.*

Breath—the way the Shofar blower calls out and sends up our prayers on our behalf.

Breath—the access point to our souls, to God.

Breath—the gateway to life on earth.

Breath—the portal to consciousness.

Breath—the moment in which we can welcome Mashiach *now*.

Breath—the key to presence, which enables gratitude, which enables joy.

And this not only answers 'what now'?,' but also 'now what?' Why? Sukkot is on the horizon!

So what?

## Notes

1. My own interpretations of the Torah lead me to believe that every time one of our forefathers said, "Hineini," (to Avraham, Moses and the other 178 times the word appears) was an indication of their conscious presence. Also, in Exodus 24:12-18, My interpretation of God telling Moses to 'go up the mountain and stay/be there' feels like an instruction to get present. See my dear friend Madison Margolin's book "Exile & Ecstasy" for more examples of presence in the Jewish tradition.

# Sukkot—Last Teaching and All You Need to Know

I will close with a story that I love. A story about the famous Rabbi Hillel the Elder on the holiday of Sukkot.[1] He was known to be very, very humble. He was in his Sukkah with his students celebrating, and he made a seemingly crazy statement. He announced, "If I am here, everything is here, and if I am not here, nothing is here." The students were startled at the arrogance. This didn't sound like their humble Rabbi. After a few whispers amongst each other, they decided to just ask the Rabbi what he meant by that.

Rabbi Hillel explained, 'It is very simple. If I am present in this Sukkah, I have everything. Everything is here with me. But if I am not present, I have nothing, nothing is here.' It is like the moment when you are on a beautiful vacation but you are in a fight with your spouse… you can't even see the gorgeous view nor taste the piña colada, you have nothing, nothing is there. Or on the other hand, you could be in a dirty alley with no plans hysterically laughing with your best friend. In that moment you have everything, everything is there. He was giving them deep instruction about how to fulfill the *mitzvah* of

Shofar Floating in the Dead Sea

## Sukkot—Last Teaching and All You Need to Know

Sukkot, which is joy. And in order to reach joy we must first be present. Right here in the now.

Mashiach *now*.

For my final blessing I just bless you and me that whenever we see or hear a Shofar that we allow it to take us right back into this present moment. That we breathe and be. And may all of that presence pave the way for the deepest gratitude for God and all He has Created from the First Shofar to the Last. And may that bring such tremendous joy that we dance all the way back to the Temple... now!

## Notes

1. Talmud Sukkah 53a.

# Nili's Famous Practical Guide to Doing Basic Tshuva!

We talk a big game about doing *tshuva*, *(and maybe you even read a whole book about it...)* but what about doing the practical *avoda*? What about actually doing the work to change?

For years my career was teaching Torah in formal institutions, and my personal life was all-Judaism, all-the-time. My head was buried in the sands of an obsessive *tshuva* routine, and I completely missed the fact that most people don't have endless hours to sit in contemplation, nor the background knowledge to even know where to begin.

So I have broken down the *tshuva* process into a handful of practical steps that can really help a person get some good personal work done, without feeling overwhelmed and lost. In the last 10 years it has spread far and wide all over the internet, and every year I get inundated with requests for the guide. SO! Here it is!

Don't worry, it's actually quite fun! I like to divide the process into a week's worth of days, dedicating a couple hours to each sit. The days do not have to be one after the next, I just divided the work into days so that you can schedule your Elul time effectively.

Shofar at the Venice Skate Park

## Nili's Famous Practical Guide to Doing Basic Tshuva!

*Tshuva* is arguably THE foundation of the world and the most profound personal growth process that was created by God even before the world was created.[1] The guide below is a tiny fraction of the process, sort of like *'Diet-Tshuva,'* but it is a great way to begin. It is also really rewarding to show up to synagogue on Rosh Hashanah knowing you put in a good effort despite how busy life can be!

The basic components of *tshuva*,[2] according to Rabbi Yitzchak Ginsburgh, are:

- Having 'Godly sorrow' for our sin.
- Confessing our sins out loud.
- Turning away from sins (with God's help).
- Choosing holiness every day.

Going through the process of true *tshuva* is quite literally why we are here as humans, is the work of a lifetime, with depths and heights that have no limits, and with boundaries that will continue to expand as long as we live. So let's start small.

Flip the page to see a map of how it's done, then we'll dive into the details.

# Nili's Tshuva Journey Map
The 6-Day Spiritual Transformation

🚀 *Begin Your Inner Journey*

**DAY 1:**
**The Sacred Notebook**

📓 Choose a special dedicated notebook
- This becomes your vessel for transformation
- Physical writing creates deeper engagement

**DAY 2:**
**Your Year in Review**

📱 Photo Journey - rediscover your year's moments

📅 Life Map - trace your calendar's story

★ Honor Growth - celebrate your wins first!

〰 Notice Patterns - acknowledge growth opportunities

✨ *Four Pillars of Tshuva:*

💧 Godly sorrow (sweet regret)

🗣 Confession (speaking aloud)

🚫 Turning away from harm

✅ Daily choosing holiness

**DAY 3:**
**The Connection Lists**

🙏 Gratitude Map - who deserves your thanks?

💌 Healing Connections - who awaits your apology?

💰 Financial Clearing - what debts need settling?

🧠 Inner Work Notes - what needs processing?

184

### DAY 4:
### Brave Communications

- 📞 Schedule meaningful conversations
- Plan texts, calls & coffee dates
- Book a therapy session for deeper wounds
- 🌳 Plan your nature conversation with God

*Set yourself up for success... call a buddy or ask your partner if they want to do Tshuva in tandem... it helps to go through the process with someone else!*

### DAY 5:
### The Power of Giving

- Charity literally 'saves from death'
- Give until your comfort zone stretches
- 🪙 Transform money into life force
- Start with those in your immediate circle

### DAY 6:
### The Heart Letter

- ✍ Write to your closest person
- Be vulnerable, specific, and loving
- Acknowledge both gifts and hurts
- Create space for profound connection

*🌈 Soul Renewed for the New Year!*

✏ **Remember:**
- Life is a journey, not a destination.
- Be gentle with yourself.
- Every step counts.

Awesome Blast

### DAY 1—GET A NOTEBOOK:

Buy or designate a notebook. I highly recommend that this notebook is only for your *tshuva* process and not a shared notebook with to-do-lists or journals. Make it special. Why? *Because you're special!* And what we do informs our own psyche of our beliefs. 'Special notebook' mentally translates into the fact that there is special hope for the one to whom said special notebook belongs.

I do not recommend doing it on your computer. There is therapeutic value in using a pen and paper, and holding your work in your hands. Still, if you know yourself and you will actually do the process on a computer rather than with a notebook, go for it. Type away baby.

Shofar in Tekoa Dalet

Nili's Famous Practical Guide to Doing Basic Tshuva!

## DAY 2—REMEMBERING WHAT YOU DID THIS YEAR!

(Recommended time: 3 hours)

Make LIST #1! This is the biggest chunk of 'work' and will lay the foundations for the rest of the process.

a. PICTURE PARTY! Look through the pictures on your phone from the year. *This part can be so fun!* Make a bullet point for each thing you want to note. Because how do you reflect on the year when you don't even remember what happened? If you are the super organized type you can leave space between each line in case you want to add anything in later.

*But Nili, I am not a picture taker... What should I do?* You can refer to your social media to see what people tagged you in!

b. CALENDAR REVIEW! Look through your calendar and jot down the different events and happenings from the past year. I go through my pictures and my calendar because I enjoy the process and I enjoy being thorough. Do what works for you.

c. A TIME FOR HOLY PRIDE! Put a star next to all of the bullet points you are proud of yourself for! Growth is not only founded on what we want to change, but what we are proud of ourselves for! This is a crucial part of the process. When we feel good about ourselves, we have more inspiration to keep going.

Here's a tip from my therapy practice: when we notice what resources it took us to accomplish things, we see what qualities are in our personal treasury that we 'own' and can use again in the future. For example, if you quit your job because

Shofar in Park Alona

ב"ה

### List #1: Things I did this year

- Hosted Rosh Hashana meal
- High Holidays at both of the Jaffa synagogues
- Met my new friends Rinat and Kaley
- ★ Made a beautiful opalescent Sukkah
- Went sukkah hopping with friends in Yaffo, so fun
- ~ Had a tiff with my landlord
- ★ Starting swimming at the beach

Keep looking through your pictures and calendar to make this very simple bullet list! After you finish the list, add stars where you are proud of yourself, and squiggly lines where Tshuva work might be available!

This list will likely take a few pages if you really jot down everything from your photos and calendar... but its fun!

it wasn't good for you, that required bravery! If you embody bravery, then it's yours, and you can do it again! And so it goes with all of our emotional resources. So we stay in balance by not only noticing opportunities for growth, but also ways we behaved or things we did that were just really great. And note that we *first* look at what we are proud of. *You're freaking awesome dude. The whole world was literally created just for YOU.*[3]

## LOOKING AT YOUR 'GOOD' BEFORE YOUR 'BAD' COMES FROM A DEEP KABBALISTIC IDEA ABOUT THE TREE OF LIFE AND THE TREE OF KNOWLEDGE.

Morah Leah Golomb taught from Reb Shlomo Carlebach that God actually did intend for Adam and Eve to eat from the Tree of Knowledge... but not yet! First they were meant to taste Shabbat,[4] to taste from the Tree of Life, and only after that would they be able to handle eating from the Tree of Knowledge. What does this mean? Let's use a modern example. If a person is new to Judaism, and they recite a certain prayer wrong, what should you do? Well, according to 'Tree of Knowledge' thinking, you could just tell them that they got the words wrong. You *know* for certain they got it wrong, it is not pronounced like that. They said it wrong, they have been saying it wrong, so it would be 'good' to correct them. But the question is, will telling them cause them to feel more alive, or cause them to feel like they want to die?

The lesson that Reb Shlomo was trying to illustrate is that in any situation in life, before we use our knowledge, and consult with the Tree of Knowledge, we must first consult with what will bring life, aliveness, and enlivening vibes... aka the Tree of Life.

## Awesome Blast

*What good is knowledge if it is going to bring death to the world? WOW. Now that is some good life advice.*

d. A TIME FOR CRINGY AWKWARDNESS! Put a squiggly line next to all of the bullet points that reminded you of things that you are less-than-proud of. A relationship gone sour, an event that flopped, a fight with a partner, a family celebration that was tense, a time you didn't take care of yourself... just note any bullet point that made you cringe a little or feel awkward. Humility begins here. The more we come clean with what needs to be cleaned up, the better we will feel going into the New Year. Life is a learning process and 'we are but dust and ashes.'[5]

e. "ASHAMNU" EXERCISE FOR THE 'A' STUDENTS. The *Machzor*, the High Holiday prayer book, has a list of sins that we confess out loud during services. We chant the list as we gently strike our chests over our hearts with closed fists, symbolizing our regret and the heart-felt pain these behaviors may have caused. Reciting this list always felt like I was reading outdated Bible-speak language that I couldn't relate to, so I decided to sit with the list in advance of the holidays, and write out how I might have actually transgressed each of these ideas. I go through the whole list, writing my own transgressions out, and then I bring my list into synagogue and read it as we sing the prayer. It makes for a way more personalized and authentic *tshuva* experience for me.

Here is the list of words that we recite.[6] You can use your *tshuva* journal to personalize each one:

אָשַׁמְנוּ. *Ah-sham-noo*. We are guilty. We have trespassed against God and man, and we are devastated by our guilt. This could even mean being guilty of not taking care of ourselves or not forgiving ourselves. What are you guilty of?

# Nili's Famous Practical Guide to Doing Basic Tshuva!

בָּגַדְנוּ. *Bah-gahd-noo.* We have betrayed God and man, we have been ungrateful for the good done to us. Have we betrayed ourselves?

גָּזַלְנוּ. *Gah-zahl-noo.* We have stolen. This can imply even the tiniest things like stealing a pen from a store or keeping your friend's borrowed clothes for longer than they would like. This can also imply symbolic stealing, like stealing someone's time by cutting in line or traffic, or stealing dignity, if you embarrassed someone, or made fun of them. This can even mean stealing content online or using illegal streaming services.

דִּבַּרְנוּ דֹּפִי. *Dee-bar-noo Doh-fee.* We have slandered. This could mean against friends, institutions, groups of people, leaders, or even politicians.

הֶעֱוִינוּ. *Heh-eh-vee-noo.* We have caused others to sin. Sometimes we have been a bad influence in the name of fun, or in the name of 'their ex deserved it,' but maybe now with a little time and space we can think about how we can be better influences?

וְהִרְשַׁעְנוּ. *Vih-heer-shah-noo.* We have caused others to commit sins for which they are called רְשָׁעִים, wicked.

זַדְנוּ. *Zahd-noo.* We have sinned with malicious intent. This is a hard pill to swallow, but we can usually find even a tiny corner of our hearts that wasn't purely innocent.

חָמַסְנוּ. *Chah-mahss noo.* We have forcibly taken. Or simply, we have been violent in our words or actions, or perhaps even in our driving or our online comments and criticisms.

טָפַלְנוּ שֶׁקֶר. *Tah-fahl-noo sheh-kehr.* We have added falsehood upon falsehood; We have joined with evil individuals or groups. We have promoted lies. Are you certain of all of the ideologies and news stories you spread this year?

## Awesome Blast

**יָעַצְנוּ רָע**. *Ya'atznoo rah*. We have given harmful advice.

**כִּזַּבְנוּ**. *Kee-zahv-noo*. We have deceived.

**לַצְנוּ**. *Lahtz-noo*. We have mocked. Ooh. Mockery, teasing, laughing at, condescension, arrogance, they all have room for a good look here. Often times we do this even while we are watching TV!

**מָרַדְנוּ**. *Mah-rahd-noo*. We have rebelled against God and His Torah. Or we have rebelled in general against parents, friends, authorities, etc.

**נִאַצְנוּ**. *Nee-ahtz-noo*. We have caused God to be angry with us.

**סָרַרְנוּ**. *Sah-rahr-noo*. We have turned away from God's Torah.

**עָוִינוּ**. *Ah-vee-noo*. We have sinned deliberately.

**פָּשַׁעְנוּ**. *Pah-shah-noo*. We have been negligent in our performance of the commandments.

**צָרַרְנוּ**. *Tzah-rahr-noo*. We have caused grief. This can include parents, siblings, clients, friends, and teachers.

**קִשִּׁינוּ עֹרֶף**. *Kee-shee-noo oh-rehff*. We have been stiff-necked, refusing to admit that our suffering is caused by our own sins. This can also imply stubbornness and unwillingness to see other people's perspectives.

**רָשַׁעְנוּ**. *Rah-shah-noo*. We have committed sins for which we are called **רָשָׁע**, raising a hand to hit someone. Or simply, we have behaved in evil ways.

**שִׁחַתְנוּ**. *Shee-chaht-noo*. We have committed sins which are the result of moral corruption.

**תִּעַבְנוּ**. *Tee-ahv-noo*. We have committed sins which the Torah refers to as abominations. Abominations can also be correlated

## Nili's Famous Practical Guide to Doing Basic Tshuva!

with desires, impulsive behaviors to get things I just desire, or things I am willing to do at the expense of myself or others.

תָּעִינוּ. *Tah-ee-noo*. We have gone astray, perhaps even from our own souls, our own talents, our own creativity, our own integrity, morals, etc.

תִּעְתָּעְנוּ. *Teeht-ah-noo*. We have led others astray.

EXTRA CREDIT FOR THE A+ STUDENT:

The list of '*Ashamnus*' is followed up by an additional list that I also like to personalize:

1. For the sins I committed under pressure
2. For hardheartedness
3. For unintentional sins
4. For sins of the lips/speech
5. For immorality
6. For sins I did openly or secretly
7. For deceiving someone
8. For improper thoughts
9. For a gathering of lewdness
10. For insincere Tshuva
11. For disrespect of teachers and parents or anyone
12. For proud looks
13. For casting off Halacha
14. For passing judgment
15. For scheming against someone

**Awesome Blast**

16. For a begrudging eye
17. For lack of seriousness (I would add the opposite)
18. For running to do evil
19. For tale-bearing/ gossip
20. For swearing in vain
21. For baseless hatred
22. For embezzlement
23. For confusion of the heart

### Nili's Famous Practical Guide to Doing Basic Tshuva!

## DAY 3—THANKS & APOLOGIES

(Recommended time: 2-3 hours.)

Precious opportunities for healing, loving, reconnection, gratitude & growth...

Using the list we made on day 2, create a list of 'Thank Yous.' Earlier, we made sure to list ways we were proud of ourselves before starting to look for ways to improve. Similarly, we want to make our list of people we would like to thank before looking at who we would like to apologize to.

If *tshuva* is all about reconnecting with ourselves, others, and God, then surely a really positive way to accomplish that is also through thanks and acknowledgment. So go through your list of what you did this year, and make List #2, which is simply a list of people you want to thank or acknowledge for specific kindnesses or general contributions to your year or life.

Later we will use this list to create a schedule of reaching out through text, voice note, email, calls and meetings. Not only will this create opportunities for connection & reconnection, but it can also fill us up with gratitude, which is a healthy and wonderful vibration that will attract more vibrations of goodness into our lives for the year to come. It's a double whammy of goodness. *Just kidding! It's actually a TRIPLE whammy of goodness* because acknowledging other people's kindnesses can often inspire us to do acts of kindness and service AND show up for others (as was done for us) where we may have previously shied away.

Shofar on the Jerusalem Underground Escalators

## Awesome Blast

If you want to be even more thorough, after you review List #1, you can also look through all of your phone or WhatsApp contacts and write down anyone you missed that you wish to thank.

Using List #1, create a list of apologies. But it's not just apologies... it's also forgiveness, financial clean ups, clearing the air, and notes for yourself for future therapy session ideas. Typically when we think about *tshuva*, we ask ourselves, 'ok, who do I need to apologize to?' but cleaning out our hearts is so much more nuanced than that.

So on my apology list I take note of if I need to pay anyone back, if there just might be some tension in any of my relationships, and also if any of the events of the year and any of my relationships could use some good processing on my part.

Later we will use this list to create a schedule of reaching out through text, voice note, email, calls and meetings, and actually paying people back.

Not only can doing this clear the air and help us reconnect with others, but it also invites us into courage and creates a vessel for your own self-esteem. As my friend Shaindel taught me, self-esteem comes from doing esteemable acts.

You could easily sweep things under the rug, but when you muster the strength to address the hard things, to confront things in kindness, you open a window to be so proud of yourself, to gain self-esteem, and to inspire others through reaching out in vulnerability. *You got this!*

ב"ה

## List #2: Thanks and Apologies

THANKS—

— Lotan and Efrat welcomed me so warmly into their home for Rosh Hashana

— Shira Sasson helped me find and organize my meals

— Victoria Khaimov and Shira Geula helped me decorate the Sukkah...

APOLOGIES—

— I yelled at the old lady who wanted my parking spot

— I communicated unkindly to...

Keep going with the thanks... it's so inspiring to see how kind people were to us this year!

and keep going with the apologies... you've got this!

Awesome Blast

## DAY 4—SCHEDULING CALLS, MESSAGES & MEETINGS

(Recommended time: 1-2 hours.)

Scheduling calls and messages: Pull out your calendar and schedule days on which to call people for thanks or apologies. If it is bound to be a longer conversation, today is the day to reach out and see when you can speak and schedule that.

I start scheduling from the beginning of Elul to make sure I don't end up in a time crunch before the holidays. Reminder, there is no rush here. Obviously it feels best to take care of all of this before Rosh Hashanah, but if it takes you more time, at least you are still committing to do it! Remember, there is no end to *tshuva*. Please do all of this work while being kind to yourself. Putting pressure or guilt onto the situation will not help you heal.

Some conversations will need sensitivity and a real phone call or coffee date. And some thanks and apologies are smaller. For the smaller ones I recommend getting right to it and shooting out a bunch of text messages on scheduling day. "I really enjoyed that Shabbat meal, and felt so grateful that you thought to include me." "Thanks so much for bringing me soup when I was sick, it really helped me." Or, "sorry for the time I embarrassed you at the party when I said..." "Sorry that I forgot your birthday."

**Scheduling therapy:** Some events and relationships might be so challenging or painful that it might be unwise to address them without prior counsel, or might be unwise to 'deal with them' at all right now if it feels emotionally

Shofar on a Horse

### Nili's Famous Practical Guide to Doing Basic Tshuva!

unsafe or if the other party involved is not open to reconciliation. Please be discerning, your emotional well-being is your most precious resource.

For these 'biggies' I like to book a few therapy sessions for myself to help me handle any unresolved feelings and emotions, and to help navigate what can and can't be done to bring healing. Sometimes, the circumstances of our lives do not allow for closure, or the hurt is too deep, and in these cases we can give ourselves space and time to process with the help of a professional or a friend. But proactively scheduling therapy, asking a friend or family member for an ear, or even making time to journal or meditate is doing what you can, and that is awesome. *Then we release control, and surrender to the flow.*

Here are 3 songs that really helped me work on releasing that might accompany you nicely through this part of the journey:

"I Release Control" by Alexa Sunshine Rose

"I Release All Things" by Beautiful Chorus

"Ho'oponopono" by the Emmit Sisters

**Scheduling a *Hitbodedut*[7] session right before Rosh Hashanah:** *Hitbodedut* is the practice of getting outside to nature, or somewhere where you have total privacy, and speaking out loud with God. Total privacy is important in case you need to cry, laugh, shout, or even scream. You want to be able to feel free to release whatever comes up.

If it will be your first time doing *hitbodedut*, then I recommend getting out for an hour (which means scheduling in drive-time on either side of the *hitbodedut*). *Yes, it can be super awkward to start talking out loud to God, but it is one of the most*

## Awesome Blast

*transformative practices I know of.* You can start by simply saying "hi God." You can begin with gratitude. You can use your lists. But essentially it's an opportunity to take all of the reflection you have done with yourself and others, and talk it out with the One who is in Charge of all of it, and Who will be co-Creating your life with you for next year! Whatever you do, don't stop speaking out loud the whole time. *Bring a pack of tissues, you might need them!*

I like to do it the day before Erev Rosh Hashanah, or on Erev Rosh Hashanah itself if I am not hosting. If you are a regular at practicing *hitbodedut*, then give yourself the time you need.

Nili's Famous Practical Guide to Doing Basic Tshuva!

## DAY 5—GIVING CHARITY AND SORTING OUT MONEY MATTERS!

(Recommended time: 1-2 hours.)

Let's get real. The work of preparing for the New Year is tantamount to asking God to save us and our loved ones from death, and to give us another year of life. Proverbs 10:2 and 11:4 say that "charity saves from death."

In fact, this promise is so real, that God even challenges us to test Him in this department! Giving charity is so powerful for so many reasons, but here in particular because our money is comparable with the life force that it took to acquire that money. If we are willing to give of our life force energy to help another, God is willing to give us life force in return.

So today is the day. Get online, bust out your credit card, and give. Give and give and give and give again. *How much? Til' it hurts. Then give again.*

I personally cannot fathom going into synagogue on Rosh Hashanah without having taken this action. It takes a ton of courage... but by now you might have noticed a theme. Everything that has to do with true *tshuva* and truly growing requires mustering more courage than you ever believed you could possess. But if we are asking for God to go beyond His Nature and give us miracles,[8] then we too must go beyond ourselves. I believe in you.

There are plenty of guidelines in the Jewish tradition as to how to give charity, but in short, try to give to those closest to you and to your community first. And of course, it also makes

Shofar overlooking Meron

## Awesome Blast

sense to give contributions to the places in which you intend to pray daily or for High Holiday services.

And as long as we are on the topic of money and trusting God, now is the time to make sure that you have settled accounts, professionally and personally. Do you owe anyone money? Did someone work for you and you forgot to pay them? Did you borrow from someone, or someone covered you at a meal when your card didn't work? I often send a text to my closest friends or people I interact with the most just to check in as close acquaintances often have plenty of money exchanges over the course of the year. I also like to walk through my house and look at all of my possessions, go into my closet and drawers and make sure I don't have anything that doesn't belong to me, or if I do, to communicate my desire to return it with the true owner.

### Nili's Famous Practical Guide to Doing Basic Tshuva!

## DAY 6—WRITING A LETTER

(Recommended time: 1-2 hours)

There is one more practice which is *mamash* the deepest. It is not sourced in our tradition, but it is sourced in love. Write a letter. A deep one. If you are married, it would be to your spouse. If you have kids and can carve out extra time, you could write them letters as well. It could be to your mom. Choose someone. Or two people if you can manage. The person you live with or are closest to. Why?

This is the person who puts up with us the most! Who does the most for us! Who drives us the most crazy! Who *we* drive the most crazy! Who we show our ugliest, worst, most monstrous, abusive, gross selves to. And no matter what state the relationship is in, there is A TON to thank them for, and A TON to acknowledge, and A TON to apologize for.

Get as detailed as possible. This letter can transform marriages, relationships, and create entirely new possibilities for repair and connection in the year ahead.

Shofar in front of the Cave of Elijah the Prophet

ב"ה

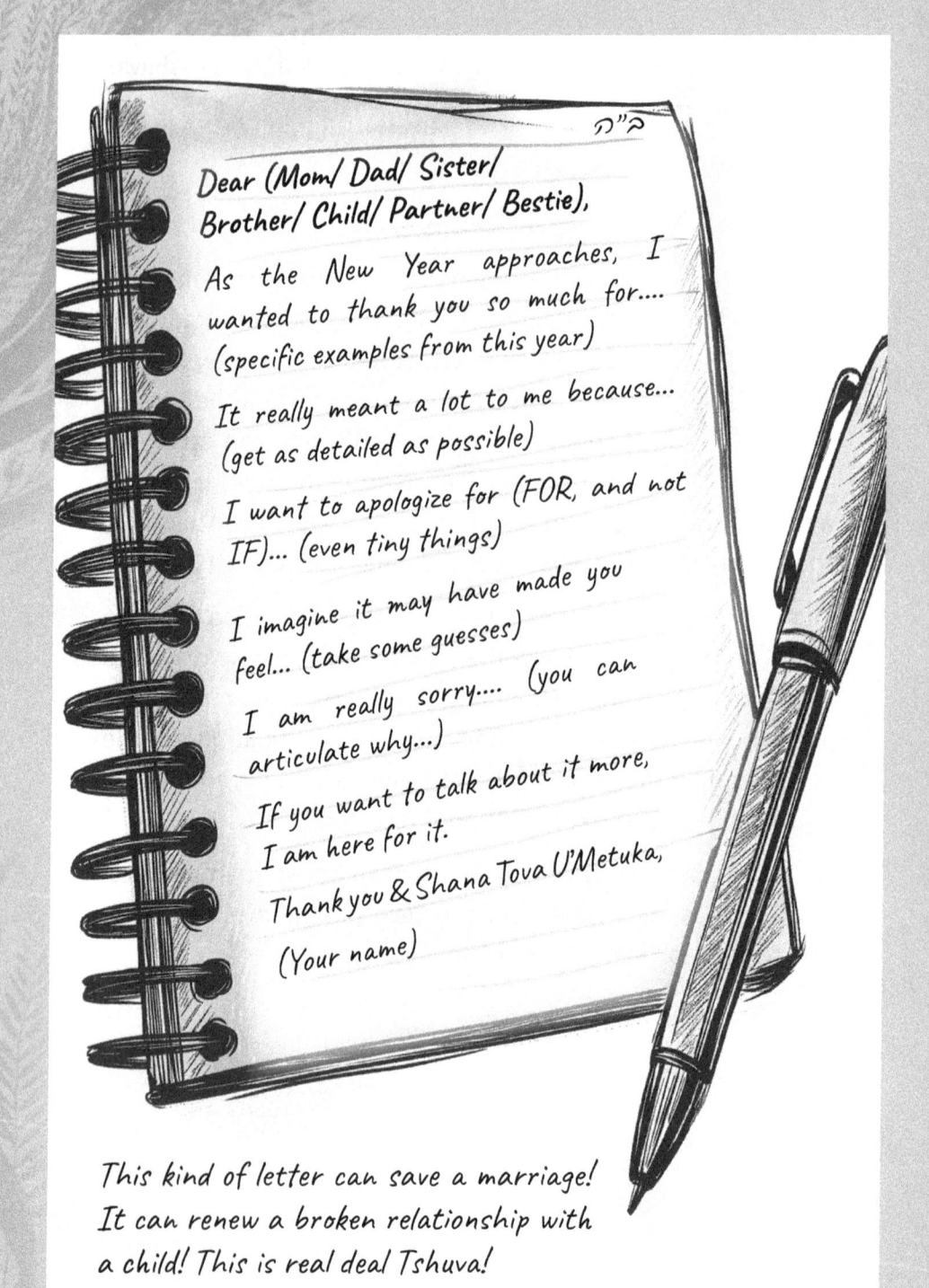

Dear (Mom/ Dad/ Sister/ Brother/ Child/ Partner/ Bestie),

As the New Year approaches, I wanted to thank you so much for.... (specific examples from this year)

It really meant a lot to me because... (get as detailed as possible)

I want to apologize for (FOR, and not IF)... (even tiny things)

I imagine it may have made you feel... (take some guesses)

I am really sorry.... (you can articulate why...)

If you want to talk about it more, I am here for it.

Thank you & Shana Tova U'Metuka,

(Your name)

This kind of letter can save a marriage! It can renew a broken relationship with a child! This is real deal Tshuva!

We forget how little we communicate with the people we love the most. So why not... start with just one truly meaningful letter this year.

Nili's Famous Practical Guide to Doing Basic Tshuva!

## BONUS *TSHUVA* RESOURCES

The Sedona Method, Reflection Questions

**The Sedona Method:** A tremendously helpful method for practicing release is employing the "Sedona Method."[9] I find it most effective to practice in partnership, alternating the role of facilitator and participant. Of course, it will be most effective with a partner you deeply trust.

1. Think of a challenging interaction about which you feel unpleasant emotions, usually connected to the experience of resentment.

2. Close your eyes and allow the emotions of resentment to be free and fill up your body. (This can get intense.)

3. Ask yourself/your partner, on a scale of 1-10 how much resentment do I/you feel? Give it a number without thinking. It's just a way to measure how the resentment shifts and releases upon practicing the exercise on repeat.

4. Ask yourself: Can a human being let go of an emotion? (Answer, Yes)

5. Ask yourself: If you knew that you could, would you? (Answer, Yes)

6. Ask yourself: if so, when would you do that? (Answer, Now)

7. Repeat the exercise until you feel the desired level of release.

What is particularly fascinating about this method is that the questions offered already have predicted universal answers. The brilliance behind this exercise is that it uses our rational thinking capacities to help us release.

## Awesome Blast

You might meet resistance and discomfort, and that is exactly why *tshuva* is such a brave practice.

**Reflection Questions:** I can't help it, I fan-girl for *tshuva*. I can't get enough and I never have enough time to dive in on my own. So I love to use any time I have in Elul when I am hanging out with friends or eating Shabbat meals to ask and answer reflection questions. I like making a game out of it and asking people to choose a number 1-50 and then they get the corresponding question to answer. Alternatively, you can use them as journal prompts. Here are some of my favorite questions that I have collected over the years. Enjoy!

1. From 1-10 how do you feel overall about this past year? About yourself?
2. What were some of your most memorable days and why? (You can use your list of what you did this year!)
3. What were the most significant events of the past year?
4. How are you different this year than last year?
5. Is there anything you did this year that you think you will remember for the rest of your life?
6. What are some things that you accomplished that you are proud of?
7. Is there a personality trait you developed a bit?
8. What are the three most important things you learned this year?
9. In what area do you feel you made your biggest improvements?
10. What do you look forward to achieving next year?

## Nili's Famous Practical Guide to Doing Basic Tshuva!

11. Is there something that was hard for you at the beginning of the year but now is not?
12. What is something you taught someone this year?
13. What is something you learned from someone this year?
14. What is the nicest thing you did for someone this year?
15. What is the nicest thing someone did for you this year? Did you thank them?
16. What was the best piece of creativity, writing, or art you did this year?
17. Who made the biggest impact on your life this year?
18. Who were your top five closest friends/people this year? Are you happy about that? Ready for any changes?
19. Did you complete anything? Release anything?
20. What did you do right? What do you feel especially good about?
21. What would be your greatest contribution this year?
22. What are six adjectives you would use to describe your year?
23. What words of wisdom, comfort or advice would you give to your former self knowing what you know now?
24. What are 1-3 goals you have for the upcoming year?
25. What blessing would you give yourself for the upcoming year?
26. How are you different this year from last year?
27. For what are you particularly grateful?
28. Is there anything you learned about yourself this year?

## Awesome Blast

29. What was your childhood dream for yourself? Do you want that to come back into your life?
30. How do you feel about your job this year? Do you want to keep it? Ditch it? Do you have a dream job?
31. How do you feel about how you spent your time this year? On social media? Any boundaries you want to set there?
32. What compliments would you give yourself for how you lived life this year?
33. If you could give yourself permission to live, feel or be any way, to release anything, what permission would you give yourself?
34. How was your relationship with God this year?
35. How was your relationship with yourself this year?
36. What is the most important part of your life?
37. What is the most special part of your life?
38. What if "anything" is possible? What would you do differently?
39. What practices did you practice that were very authentic to who you truly are?
40. What would falling in love with yourself look like? Being your own biggest cheerleader? Does anything prevent you from doing that?
41. What do you want to look back on at the end of life (after 120) and say that you did/were?
42. If tonight was your last night on earth what would you tell the people you love, to yourself? To Hashem?

### Nili's Famous Practical Guide to Doing Basic Tshuva!

43. What was the most challenging part of the year for me and how did I/you face it?

44. What are some things or qualities that I/you want to improve on next year?

45. Are there any regrets? Is there a healthier way to address those feelings?

46. What is something you feel unresolved about but would like to feel a little or a lot better about?

47. What are some areas of life you could really use some self-compassion for?

48. If you could wave a magic wand and change some areas of your life, what would you change?

49. In which ways do you feel that your behavior was inauthentic to who you truly are?

50. How can you offer yourself understanding for these challenging parts?

THAT'S ALL FOLKS! YOU SLAYED TSHUVA! And remember, this process is one to be done with love and gentleness. Life is busy and we are all trying our best. Do what you can, celebrate your efforts, and then give yourself permission to release on the rest... life is a journey and we are works in progress! But hey, you got this far! WOOOOHOO!!!! Go team. And on behalf of the Nation of Israel and the world, we thank you for your personal contributions to elevating yourself and thereby bringing us all closer to the Great Day!

Awesome Blast

## Notes

1. Breishit Raba 1:4.
2. The laws of tshuva are explained at large in Rambam's famous "Hilchot Tshuva" and are way too vast to present here.
3. Gemara Sanheidrin 37.
4. Tasting Shabbat implies having a taste of the World to Come, where everything is One, and where there is no distinction or judgment of 'good' and 'bad.'
5. Gemara Sanheidrin 37.
6. Hebrew and English text adapted and taken from The Metsudah Machzor, via Sefaria.
7. Mei HaShiloach, Volume I, Genesis, Chayei Sara 4, Likutei Moharan 52:5:1-4, From David to Destruction, Eliyahu HaNavi and the Drought of Faith, A Fed Up Man of Faith 11, Likutei Tefilot, Volume II 11:1-7.
8. Rabbanit Yemima Mizrachi.
9. Here I must give my dad a shout out as he didn't stop talking about the Sedona Method for my entire childhood, lol! Thanks dad, you're such a cool trendsetter, ahead of the game!

# Further Resources

NILI's LINK TREE

aka how to connect to Nili's Social Media, Psychotherapy Website, Music Videos & more:

linktr.ee/nilisalem

STAY TUNED!

Nili & Shira Geula's new song "Everything is Always Working Out for Me" is coming out soon!

# Dictionary of Hebrew Words

**Ado-nai**—my Lord aka a way we reference God in our prayers

**Aggadah**—the non-legalistic exegesis which appears in the classical rabbinic literature of Judaism, particularly the Talmud and Midrash

**Akeida**—the Binding of Isaac

**Aliyah**—the modern day term for when a Jew in the diaspora returns to the Land of Israel to live, literally, 'a going up'

**Amidah**—The central prayer of the Jewish prayer service

**Ani LeDodi VDodi Li**—I am for my Beloved and my Beloved is for me

**Aruch HaShulchan**—A book of Jewish law

**Ashkenazi/m**—Jews who descend people who lived in Central or Eastern Europe

**Avodah**—literally work, but here it references spiritual service

**Baal Tokea**—the one who is chosen to sound the Shofar at the High Holidays

**Baruch shekivanti**—an expression used to convey gratitude or excitement in recognizing that you had a Torah idea from your own heart or mind that was

Shofar in Gan Soccer

Dictionary of Hebrew Words

also brought down and validated by an earlier sage or scholar, without your knowing it previously to it coming down to you as well.

**Beit Din**—court of Jewish Law

**Bina**—Understanding, also one of the Kabbalistic Divine emanations, aka *sfirot*

**Bitoosh**—the Baal Shem Tov's spiritual practice of hammering heart for surrender

**Chabad**—a sect of Chassidic Judaism

**Chachna'ah**—Surrender

**Chaggim**—Literally holidays. A phrase used in Judaism to describe the full process of Rosh Hashanah, Yom Kippur and Sukkot.

**Chassidut**—Teachings of the Kabbalah, distilled and elaborated on by Jewish mystics

**Chas VeShalom**—an expression that means God forbid

**Chesed**—Kindness or lovingkindness, also one of the Kabbalistic Divine emanations, aka *sfirot*

**Cheshbon HaNefesh**—A spiritual accounting of the soul

**Chick-Chak**—an expression that means quickly

**Chiddush/im**—New insight/s

**Chukat**—a portion of the weekly Torah readings

**Chuppah**—the traditional Jewish wedding canopy

**Chutzpah (holy Chutzpah)**—brazenness, but often referred to in a positive/bold/courageous sense

**Daven**—pray in Yiddish

## Awesome Blast

**Dreidel**—the toy we spin on Chanukah

**Ein Od Milvado**—the expression that means there is nothing else but God

**Emunah**—faith/ trust in God

**Elul**—the month that begins the process of introspection before the New Year

**Eshel**—a specific type of tree

**Eshpoch Sichi Lefanecha**—to pour forth one's conversation/ heart before God

**Gan Eden**—the Garden of Eden, or metaphorically, a Paradisiacal state of mind

**Gehinnom**—loosely defined as 'Hell' or 'Purgatory, or metaphorically, a hellish state of mind

**Gematria**—the numerological value of a Hebrew letter, word, etc

**Gevurah**—strength/discipline, also one of the Kabbalistic Divine emanations, aka *sfirot*

**Halacha**—Jewish law

**Halachik**—is in line with Jewish law

**HaRachaman**—The Compassionate One

**Hashem**—how we reference God, literally The Name

**Haya**—the past

**Hidur Mitzvah**—beautifying a good deed

**Hineini**—here I am

# Dictionary of Hebrew Words

**Hitbodedut**—the practice of going outside by yourself to a place where you have privacy and speaking out loud with God.

**Hitchadshut**—renewal. Rebbe Nachman meant it in the sense of being willing over to start again in any moment

**Hoveh**—the present

**Katonti**—literally, I have been made small, aka humbled

**Kav**—a line, in the Kabbalistic sense, it is the place within where God created the Universe

**Kavanah**—intention (Kavanot—intentions)

**Kesef**—money

**Keter**—literally crown, but also, the highest *sfira* or energetic emanation in the Kabbalistic Tree of Life.

**Kiruv**—the work of bringing Jews closer to their Judaism, their souls, to God

**Kisufim**—longings

**Kodesh Kedoshim**—the Holy of Holies, the inner sanctum of the Temples in Jerusalem

**Kol Nidre**—the prayer service that begins Yom Kippur, literally, all the vows

**Kosher**—a term that hints at what is acceptable for a Jew to eat, or an appropriate way for a Jew to behave

**Leshaper**—to improve (something)

**LeHishtaper**—to improve oneself

**Lishmoa**—to hear/to listen

## Awesome Blast

**Mekabetz Nidchei Amo Yisrael**—He Who gathers in the dispersed of His nation of Israel

**Machzor**—the prayer book specifically designed for the High Holidays

**Mamash/Mamesh**—very, or a term that puts emphasis on anything one says

**Magen David**—the Star of David

**Mashiach**—the Messiah

**Mei Shefer**—amniotic fluid

**Midrash**—from Wikipedia: is an expansive Jewish Biblical exegesis using a rabbinic mode of interpretation prominent in the Talmud. The word itself means "textual interpretation", "study", or "exegesis", derived from the root verb *darash* (דָּרַשׁ), which means "resort to, seek, seek with care, enquire, require."

**Mishnah**—the first major written collection of the Jewish oral traditions that are known as the Oral Torah

**Mikvah**—ritual pool for spiritual service

**Minhag**—a Jewish custom

**Mitzvah**—a commandment from the Torah, also called a good deed

**Mizbe'ach**—the sacrificial altar in the Mishkan and Temple where people came to ask forgiveness and offer thanks

**Moshe Rabbeinu**—Moses our Rabbi/teacher

**Morah**—teacher (feminine)

**Na**—please

# Dictionary of Hebrew Words

**Nachash**—snake

**Neilah**—the final prayer service of Yom Kippur.

**Neshama**—soul

**Neshima**—breath

**Nidchei**—those who are dispersed, literally, those who are unrecognizable

**Olam Haba**—the World to Come

**Or Ein Sof**—the light of the Infinite

**Oy Vey**—'Oh wow' in Yiddish, but connoting, 'oh no' or, "oh this isn't good'

**Rah**—bad/ evil

**Rachamim**—compassionate

**Razton**—will/desire

**Rechem**—womb

**Rosh Hashanah**—the Jewish New Year

**Sefaradi/m**—Jews descended from those Jews who left the Iberian Peninsula

**Sfira/Sfirot**—a Divine energy channel as referenced on the Kabbalistic Tree of Life diagram, an emanation

**Shalom Bayit**—peace in the home

**Shabbas/t**—the Sabbath

**Shana Tova U'Metukah**—Happy and sweet New Year

**Shidduch (Date)**—A date with someone for the sake of finding one's marital partner. Shidduch would be technically translated as 'a match'.

## Awesome Blast

**Shiur**—Torah class/lesson

**Shlichut**—a service opportunity to help a Jewish community, often elsewhere in the world

**Shlita**—The term "Shlita" is actually an acronym, and stands for the words "*Sheyichye L'orech Yamim Tovim Aruchim.*" This means that we pray that he "will live many long and good days." As a word, "Shlita" means that the Rabbi is a person of leadership.

**Shema**—the central prayer in Judaism, "Hear oh Israel, the Lord Our God, the Lord is One." Shema, (Hebrew: "Hear"), the Jewish confession of faith made up of three scriptural texts (Deuteronomy 6:4—9, 11:13—21; Numbers 15:37—41), which, together with appropriate prayers, forms an integral part of the evening and morning services

**Shul**—Yiddish for synagogue

**Shvarim**—the Shofar blast with 9 short blasts

**Sichot HaRan**—one of the books of teachings from Rebbe Nachman

**Sitra Achra**—the 'other side' aka the side that inclines us to thinking, speaking and doing evil

**Sukkot**—a major Jewish festival held in the autumn to commemorate the sheltering of the Israelites in the wilderness.

**Stahm**—slang for 'I'm just joking,' or 'it's just a joke.'

**Talmud**—the Oral tradition in Judaism

**Tchiyat Hameitim**—the Ressurection of the Dead

# Dictionary of Hebrew Words

**Tefach**—a biblical measurement

**Tehillim**—Psalms

**Tekia/Gdola**—the Shofar blast with only one blast/ the longer version

**Tiferet**—the quality of compassion or beauty, also one of the Kabbalistic Divine emanations, aka *sfirot*

**Tishrei**—the Hebrew month which hosts the holidays of Rosh Hashanah, Yom Kippur and Sukkot

**Tfilah/Tfillot**—prayer/s

**Truah**—the Shofar blast with 3 blasts

**Tshuva**—repentance, return to self

**Tzimtzum**—contraction

**Vayichen (Ha'am)**—And the nation found favor in each others eyes, literally and they encamped

**Vort**—Yiddish for a short torah teaching.

**Yeshiva**—a institute for Torah learning

**Yichud Room**—the room a Jewish couple goes into after their wedding ceremony to 'seal the deal' that they are officially a married couple.

**Yihiyeh**—will be

**Y-K-V-K**—the English acronym for the Hebrew name of God

**Yom Kippur**—the holiday of repentance

**Yontiff**—a holy day

**Z'l**—acronym for Zichrono/ Zichrona Livracha, or may his/her memory be for a blessing

# More Shofar Videos

| | | | |
|---|---|---|---|
| [QR] | Shofar on a tractor outside Kibbutz Beeri | Shofar in a Rolls Royce, beverly hills | [QR] |
| [QR] | Shofar at Yitzhar | Shofar at Venice Beach | [QR] |
| [QR] | Shofar over the Gaza Strip | Shofar where David Slew Goliath | [QR] |
| [QR] | Shofar at Givat Nili | Shofar at the grave of Matityahu and the Maccabees | [QR] |
| [QR] | Shofar at Caesarea | Shofar at the Tomb of Isaac and Rebecca | [QR] |
| [QR] | Shofar at Nokdim | Shofar in Shuk HaCarmel, TLV | [QR] |
| [QR] | Shofar at Gan HaPa'amon | Shofar Artwork Compilation around LA | [QR] |
| [QR] | Shofar at Beit Meir | Shofar overlooking the Kotel | [QR] |

## More Shofar Videos

| | | | |
|---|---|---|---|
| [QR] | Shofar at Hebron | Shofar at a Nachlaot Party | [QR] |
| [QR] | Shofar in Modiin | Shofar at the Grave of Rav' Shlomo Carlebach | [QR] |
| [QR] | Shofar at Kinneret | Shofar in Marina Del Rey | [QR] |
| [QR] | Shofar at Silwan | Shofar at the Jaffa Port | [QR] |
| [QR] | Shofar at Sderot | Shofar on a Wall | [QR] |
| [QR] | Shofar at Shchem-Nablus | Shofar at Bat Ayin - Judaean Hills | [QR] |
| [QR] | Shofar at the Eiffel Tower | Shofar at the forest in Efrat | [QR] |
| [QR] | Shofar at the Statue of Liberty | Shofar at Damascus Gate | [QR] |
| [QR] | Shofar as Forrest Gump | Shofar in an ancient cistern in Tzfat | [QR] |
| [QR] | Shofar at the Nova Site | Shofar on a Catamaran | [QR] |
| [QR] | Shofar in the Eucalyptus Fields in Pardes Chana | Shofar in Westwood Village | [QR] |

# Awesome Blast

Shofar on a Caravan Porch in the Shomron

Shofar in Palm Springs

Shofar with the frogs in the Botanical Gardens of Jerusalem

Shofar in the Malibu Mountains

Shofar at the Neon Green Natural Spring

Shofar at a Tarzana Adar Party

Shofar in the Secret Garden in Ein Kerem

Shofar at a Sacred Song Circle

Shofar at Damascus Gate, Old City, Jerusalem

Shofar on a Party Sail Boat off Herzliya

Shofar prayer in Rome at the Colosseum

## About the Author
### Behind the Blast: A Personal Journey

*Nili Salem is an international voice of inspiration, known for her vibrant teachings in Jewish mysticism, soulful Torah storytelling, and transformational work as a spiritual psychotherapist for women, both in private practice and online.*

It all began with a short n' squawky $20 Shofar. Second-grade Nili excitedly and proudly spent every last dollar of her allowance on that little horn—and unknowingly ignited a lifetime of passion. By her twenties, she was hired by the very same synagogue that sold her the Shofar—this time as their official High Holiday Shofar Blower and Chazzanit in Beverly Hills.

Her pre-game ritual? Trips to the tanning salon, hair 'did,' sparkly kippah donned, and rainbow tallit draped just right. Mic'd up like Madonna, with a live orchestra behind her, she would belt out *Kol Nidre* like her congregation's souls were on the line. (Whisper even a hint of it to her today, and she might just give you the full cantorial rendition—on the spot!)

Each year when the High Holidays ended, Nili would head out into the world, doing field research, thesis work, and teaching among the Lost Tribes. It was a calling passed down from her mother (z"l), who had volunteered in Ethiopia the very year Nili was born.

With a slightly longer Shofar slung across her back, she journeyed across the globe—from Rwanda to Uganda,

## Awesome Blast

Zimbabwe to Zanzibar, India to Indonesia, Buenos Aires to Beijing, Tulum to Thailand, and Nicaragua to Peru. Her mission: to help usher in the prophetic dream of the Ingathering of the Exiles... and its ultimate vision—the greatest celebration ever known to humankind, at the House of Love and Prayer for All Nations. Coming soon to a Temple in Jerusalem near you.

Along the way, she pushed the limits of adventure: dropping out of university to tour with a rock band, a month-long motorcycle journey, surviving malaria and meningitis, and dancing in masked tribal ceremonies on cliffs that made the wildest of *National Geographic* episodes look tame. Layered atop these were near-death experiences, ego-shattering divorce, and a deep desire for integrity, joy, and truth. That desire led her—again and again—back to the path of spiritual return.

Since making Aliyah in 2008, Nili has immersed herself in Torah learning and Jewish mysticism, prayer, meditation, consciousness work, alternative healing, and sacred plant medicine. She believes that making space for our pain, shadows, shame, and fears is not just necessary—it's holy. In the depths, we uncover our brightest light, dormant gifts, and deepest connection to the Divine.

*Tshuva*—returning to her soul-truth, ancestral wisdom, and relationship with God—has saved her life more times than she can count. She often feels like she's won the happiness jackpot, and she credits it entirely to the gift of authentic spiritual growth work. It's that gift she now dedicates herself to sharing with others.

Nili lives and swims by the turquoise waters of Yaffo-Tel Aviv. She delights in dark chocolate, fizzy water, raucous laughter,

## About the Author

spontaneous freestyle rapping, drumming djembes, and blowing the Shofar at Sacred Song Circles.

After three years deep in study and writing, she's humbled to present *Awesome Blast*—a heartfelt guide to prepare for the Days of *Awe*, soul-healing, and spiritual return, rooted in Torah and the call of the Shofar.

**Whether teaching in international circles or guiding powerful one-on-one therapy sessions, Nili helps others awaken to the truth of who they are—with humor, courage, and compassion.**

**To invite Nili for a speaking engagement, musical event, or personalized transformational therapy package, visit www.nilibsimcha.com or email her at nilisalem@awesomeblastbook.com.**

photograph by Katie McKnoulty, Tuscany,
Inner Landscape Retreat w Alexa Eden

## Want a Shofar Like Nili's?

Bring the sound of your soul home with your very own long, handcrafted shofar—sourced straight from the heart of Jerusalem.

These are the same verified, kosher shofars used by Nili herself. Each one is unique, powerful, and ready to travel anywhere in the world—yes, we ship internationally!

Visit **awesomeblastbook.com/shofar** to order yours.

We'll walk you through everything—from size and style to care and meaning.

And yes... you're totally welcome to send us a video of your first awesome blast.

Mazal tov, Shofar Owner. You're officially one of us.

*Shofar videos optional, lol.*